REACHING IN ALL DIRECTIONS

REACHING IN ALL DIRECTIONS

John D. Wallace

REACHING IN ALL DIRECTIONS

iUniverse books may be ordered through booksellers or by contacting:

iUniverse
1663 Liberty Drive
Bloomington, IN 47403
www.iuniverse.com
1-800-Authors (1-800-288-4677)

ISBN: 978-1-5320-0494-0 (sc)
ISBN: 978-1-5320-0495-7 (hc)
ISBN: 978-1-5320-0496-4 (e)

Print information available on the last page.

iUniverse rev. date: 09/28/2016

I am the doormat
Who collects the mud on your shoes and
Forms it into a ball.
So the next time that mud pile is before you,
Just remember the ball I have made for you.
Step into the mud again if you will
Or if you cannot will against it,
But when you return to my door,
Do not be surprised
To see the doormat is gone:
Remove your shoes,
Pick off the mud, and
Have yourself a ball—
Meet me inside with bare feet.

CONTENTS

Author's Notes

FOREWORD

One might take this time to discuss the intentions behind creating such a work called, <u>Reaching *In All* Directions</u>, but in fact I only wish to say that it had no particular intention (at least to begin with) and thus serves to be a true expression of adolescent contemplations. Especially from the starting point of the beforehand, the most true and self-revealing expressions are carried through without intention. Only *afterward* can one truly come to discover where they were coming from. Enjoy!

David Manfold: Frustratingly jumps from one emotional extreme to the other – between his positive desire to speak all that he thinks and his endless **impatience** with the inadequacy of the spoken word. As he struggles to reconcile those two points of view, there is a noticeable **urgency** about the verbal expression of his inner workings. He tends to jump quickly to conclusions of world-view and so creates a personalized vocabulary that is rarely adequate to describe his fantastic notions in terms of social relevance. In trying to grasp a hold of what he imagines to be some creative force that motivates the path of everything in existence, he clings to the grandiose and mysterious idea of the "Spirit" which seems to lack clear explanation while only clouding his mind in frustration to grasp.

Prescott Bookman: Speaks with a "holy" tongue, adhering to the teaching of **general lessons**. His lessons have the ultimate objective of providing comfort to others through empathetic understanding. Relates more to the abstract than the analytical, so he at times becomes so abstract as to sound fatherly or all-knowing. Shows consistent attention to religious issues, with an overt confidence in the saving grace of Jesus Christ. This confidence is sometimes impetuously overextended to the uneasy surprise of the others.

Martin Overfield: Enjoys entertaining the realm of fantasy in thought but still shows discipline about needed boundaries. Is thoroughly entertained by pictorial representations and narrative constructions . . .from this he develops ideas in **storyline**. Understands his personal patterns and habits, as he shows an uncanny ability to remove from and reflect on the habitual self.

Jimmy Simpson: Constantly entertains the realm of fantasy – most often without first establishing direction (proudly) and with little respect for rules or creative discipline. Brings a socially resistant attitude which can be seen as a reflection of his **pending shift** from adolescence to adulthood. To prevent this shift he often regresses into capricious, childlike thinking, which brings to the discussion both benefits and impediments. His **childishness** shows itself in playfulness, games, camaraderie, and an overall unitarian spirit.

Peter Clearville: Even keeled. Rarely shows emotion but can be the most mentally engaged and focused of the group. He is constantly involved in focused observation: integrating ideas, forming intellectual frameworks, and analyzing/dissecting those frameworks. Often provides the clearest insight – acting as an **objective voice of reason**. For his own emotional stability he tends to dilute the intensity of his ideas and worldviews by breaking them down into more definitive, intellectualized terms.

IMPATIENCE

&

THE STORY BEHIND THE WORD

David: Somehow they've gotten us all here, so how about we just cut to the chase?

Jimmy: But they? Who is "they"? What about *us*? It's more like somehow *we've* gotten ourselves here, into this mess.

David: I can see you're going be the stubborn one.

Jimmy: I'm just saying – I rarely remember exactly how I come to end up in different situations, and I surely don't remember being born, so let's not pretend we know where we are or how we got here.

Martin: Do you have any idea? Do you have *any* idea? If you feel the need to know where you are, then you have no idea. You are lost in your mind.

Prescott: Home. That's my idea – the place where thoughts are welcome, and you all are welcome. When we entertain unwelcome thoughts, we feel as if we are away from home – in a place where one might ask the question: where am I? I hope we are here to join the place where thoughts are welcome. Let me be the first to say that I welcome you all.

Martin: Thanks, Prescy.

Prescott: You're welcome.

Jimmy: God, where do I begin? Things feel familiar. But if this is here, and this is home, I surely don't remember building this place.

//David initiates communication and shows his desire for the discussion to be fast and efficient in coming to its ultimate revelation/conclusion. "Cut to the chase" has double meaning under the verbal surface: He vaguely hints toward his personal conception of the universe as having some ultimate/divine purpose. At the same time he displays his personal urgency about the lack of completion about the universe, as it seems to be a process unfinished. Such "under the surface hints" exhibit David's yearning to establish unspoken/nonverbal communication, that is, there is an *unrelenting* desire to find the *next* person (all persons) who might understand/receive the unspoken. Jimmy quickly picks up on the unspecific pronoun ("they") as it clearly has no distinctions or boundaries: the first reference to *God* – no limits. Jimmy furthermore opposes the externally oriented pronoun used by David, instead calling for a sense of community ("us") in the discussion. Multiple meaning is everywhere.//

Martin: Boy, you are stubborn – full of questions. Not too shabby.

David: Stubborn? Who are you to say? Don't we all have to be stubborn about some things? If I attach and refuse to let go, they might call me stubborn, but how does one decide which moments of clarity are the ones to hold onto? Maybe there was one instance when I truly understood. I think Someone understood once and wanted to keep that time – the moment of Truth. Stubborn, maybe? But the keeper of one time is the keeper of soul—the under stander of place unity—the One who will not let go of the moment that feels complete. They may call it stubborn. **I might call it stubborn.** Nonetheless, the stubborn halt to keep the place in time.

Martin: No one would ever stop to think that our great times might end soon, or even at all . . . so much talking, laughing, permanent agreeability. . . then the moment stops. Silence kicks in . . . all is lost. That's the problem: when we seem to have found the moment, the moment stops? What next? Maybe if we're stubborn that moment will find its way back.

Prescott: Does it not feel like there is a place We all belong…as it all boils down…to that moment you speak of – some ultimate culmination of Truth revealed? In one form or another, we all possess intrinsic anticipation of an eternal state – completing the full circle of life…Love

[*The "L Word" brings a short silence to the crowd*]

Jimmy: Our lives in commune attempt to fill the ultimate awkward silence that is our muted universe – a dead silence. Is it happen-sake that we evolved to speak out with words to fill the air? Or is it that we just couldn't take the awkward silence?

Martin: The awkwardness of silence – enough said. Get it?

//David continues using indirect references and hints at his Christian predispositions by speaking of some "One who keeps the moment of Truth," i.e. Jesus. Prescott, Martin, and Jimmy all remark on the experience of some "moment that feels complete," as if to hint at some universal/communal purpose, the fulfillment of that purpose, and some resulting sense of completion. They all expect this fulfillment to involve an eternal, *communal* state of shared Truth. With respect to the fallen silence, Martin and Jimmy both recognize management of perceived social awkwardness: Jimmy describes the universe as mute or of silence, possibly implicating the irresponsive nature of "God" in there being no direct or certain line of communication.//

David: Okay, so we're talking about words. Don't get me started! Don't get the world started, Jeez . . . Us! We have defined Everything! The world is now all-powerful in the way of numbers. The Spirit has been broken down, so its presence is diluted. We cannot define Our Love through numbers, so when you define the whole world this way, sides are drawn, hate breaks through, judgments are made, and wars are fought. I want to break down these definitions and see the Spirit that produced them. So what about the quiet one? Are you going to sit there and observe or get in with Us?

//David's anxiety is outward and obvious. He refers to the typical use of language as having superficial motives. He also jumps quickly to the conclusion that language is the root of all hate and judgment, proposing that humans tend to improperly see things in terms of pieces or categories rather than as part of a more inclusive whole. "The Spirit that produced them" is David's conception of some primeval force that "produces" expressions via self-revealing semiotic structures.//

Peter: I am with you—yes—words easily inhibit. It's easy to fool oneself – this bothers me, too. I too have trouble accepting physical reality, for the very nature of the physical is inhibiting – it is that of boundaries. Often much clearer is the sight of closed eyes: I feel more certain seeing nothing at all rather than the fraction of the spectrum that my eyes permit.

[*Thoughts*]

Martin: Scenario: I am looking down at a dry bowl of cereal. I have seen it before. I recognize it. I can even *feel* what it would taste like. So what the hell is it called!? Goddam, a mind blank! A goddam mind blank! I swear I know what *it* is called. I swear I do, but I just can't remember. . . . . Ladies and Gentlemen, it is at this moment, finally this moment that I can call myself a genius of cognitive awareness. I am smarter than I have ever been.

Golden Grams! That's right! Golden Grams! I knew it! Man, that feels good!

So I tend to leave my little scenarios with a some open space for imagination. I like it this way. But I feel I should clarify about calling myself a genius at this particular moment: It is my absolute belief that not only did I have full "knowledge" of what that damn cereal was, but I had momentarily achieved a greater knowledge of the cereal. I gazed at it on a whole new level, engrossed in its qualities – not yet running to establish its name. My feeble brain just couldn't let it go: I had to know the name! I just had to know it! Next time, I'm just gonna let it go.

David: The whole of it all comes first, you know – the gestalt. It's hard to tell that split second before you start fumbling around with the names of all those pieces—you know—placing little tacks on the board, discovering new names and new shades, all to give the whole scene some semblance of permanence – purely objective, right? To say, yeah: this is this, and that is that, and WoWee – this is *how* this goes with that. But it's not this or that; it's this, that, and the other, 1-2-3, you know? They're all part one forsaken whole that you've taken apart. So here I am again in that split-second before the whole starts coming to pieces. I was thinking maybe you could do me a favor this time and recognize that split second and string it out for me, share it with me . . . then all those fumbling pieces become still . . . And we meet at last.

Jimmy: I don't think . . . we are as smart . . . as we think.

Martin: Ha Ha Ha. Exactly.

//Martin's scenario continues to entertain the discussion of language, particularly the topic of naming, as disguising to the Truth. Jimmy seconds that emotion and goes on to playfully depict a transcendent intelligence behind the gradual formation of ideas – an intelligence that is not readily conscious. In other words, Jimmy proposes that while our thoughts may have superficial ignorance (insofar as they might be irrational and/or irrelevant engagements that are immediately conscious), there remains a much greater intelligence underneath the production of these sometimes "ignorant" thoughts in terms of their underlying development.//

Prescott: Thoughts of the Church. So many words, drawn out homilies and infallible proclamations – the more human words we use to speak of God's purpose, the farther away we set ourselves from God. Take your time, and if you need a word for the time being, make it One – Love.

Martin: The ultimate failure of popular religion is the elimination of creative wonder about the concept of "God," that is, what looms underneath the single word that is supposed to label His entire essence of being. Such a One-word reference should always be growing, as it is the ultimate unclear concept perpetually evolving toward explosion into clarity...This continuous process of wonder and creative elaboration is what makes the one-word mystery of "God" such a utility to explore. *This* process, of finding the true story behind the word, is beauty. The wonder and curiosity involved in such creative expansion should carry-over to all meaningful expressions and discussions.

David: He had a need to give it a name . . . "*it*" was scary. So now we work out who is really in control . . .

Prescott: The difference between believing in **a** God and believing **in** God is the hugest. You can't skim.

Jimmy: I don't see how you can or why you do substitute the ritual for the actual experience that the ritual represents.

Prescott: Yes, be careful, or your people will seek the ritual and not the Truth of the actual experience. They will follow, indeed, but they will not follow in Truth.

Martin: They followed the emotional parade until they realized and became uncertain. Wishing of this never again, they remembered the parade and felt good. Their spirit died: now they only follow the emotional parade, having no need or desire to wonder where it's headed. So who are the schmucks at the front? Would we ever question their certainty and disrupt the parade? Certainly not.

Prescott: I listen to Catholic theologians talk of church doctrine. Peter and his rock, papal infallibility, or maybe a word of excommunication or two. I listen to this, and I cry. I cry for all of my brothers and sisters who are torn apart by human distinctions. All of the world bundles inside my heart and cries out loud.

//Prescott displays his notably forthright capacity for empathetic imagination. Minding attention to religious issues he continues to entertain the discussion's portrayal of language, employing a biblical reference: "God is Love." Everyone follows Prescott's attention to the shortcomings of the Church by giving their own opinions. The majority of church-goers are portrayed as followers who submit to the comfort of theocratic authority without thinking for themselves. Because of such passive obedience and lack of skeptical curiosity, the Church fails to create true believers.//

Jimmy: Curiosity killed the catechism, ay?

[*Chuckles*]

David: It's the unsatisfactory explanation: whether thorough or concise, we must explain. Words can be used to explain things. At the beginning, we could explain nothing – words were our savior. But the more we use words to explain things, the farther away the curious human sets himself away from the whole point of it all – to help understand what he can't explain! Oh, how we yearn to explain the unexplainable! Is this not the Spirit? But please, don't define the Spirit. Its definition has no value in word. But still, Our words are guided, and Our story will be told. Look to music, the Spirit holder, and understand where these words come from. You will not be disappointed.

Jimmy: The Spirit is the happen-sake. If all you know is words, you'll try and label it, and you won't believe It: then . . . sake just happens.

David: Our world is numerical. The Spirit is not. As the Spirit is broken down in numbers, its definition is clouded. We must realize that numbers are false and counting is false. *Combining* is Truth. If we don't have faith in the Spirit, we will seek certainty in the tale of numbers. This certainty will blind us from the Truth, but the Spirit will remain alive, hidden, sheathed in gray. If we can see the Truth, the Spirit's sheath will be lifted, and numbers will lose all meaning. My words leave me always in disguise, but together the Truth will be told. The Spirit does not choose sides because by choosing a side you disguise what is real, and you never see the whole Truth. The Spirit sees the Truth; It does not choose sides.

//"Spirit" is almost without question the most annoyingly undefined word floating around the discussion. Nevertheless, it continues to be kicked around, delightfully accompanied by nothing more than vague distinctions. This is a testament to the playful "spirit" of the group, as it takes satisfaction in having a flexible concept they can play with, mold, and shape as they will, much like children play with a ball of play-doh. This "molding process" is a critical layer of the discussion that is sure to develop into a telling shadow of its trajectory as a whole. At the moment, David remains choppily detached in his communication: "Understand where these words come from," is his attempt to show that there is a singular nature through which all expressions originate. Jimmy plays well with this concept, using "happen-sake" as his linguistic instrument: He implies that the Spirit is the intelligent Force behind all coincidences, circumstances, and "happen-sakes" – it is the sake for which [blank] happens.//

Prescott: Yes, I intend to leave no one out. Truth is Everyone. Forgive me for throwing these words at you. I mean, I intend otherwise. The other wise intend. I intend otherwise. I offer my life . . . take it or leave it.

Martin: Nice way to play Prescott: a flashy transposition. I didn't know if you had it in you.

Prescott: So you wonder . . . Is *it* in you? Is *it* in you?? Don't ask Gatorade – that's a drink. Ask yourself.

Jimmy: Random association to Gatorade, Prescottonball! Love that kind of spark – shocks my system all the time.

Martin: And me.

David: And me.

Peter: And me.

Prescott: Of all the things We share, what if there was just one thing that We could all share as human beings but has remained elusive as of yet? And what if that one thing was the most powerful force in the universe – **the** Force if you will? That would be fun. . .

Jimmy: Yeah, **fun**! That's the spirit, Prescott! You may even call **that** the Spirit. Ha.

//Prescott shows some versatility by leaking a bit of playfulness, much to the surprise of the others. There is a distinct, communal agreement that serves the important function of raising awareness to the things they share. What appears to be a simple comment by Jimmy ("That's the spirit, Prescott! You may even call that . . .") actually demonstrates piercing awareness of the versatility of the word mechanisms used in the discussion.//

Martin: Well, before we start running around in circles – not to say that doesn't have its charm, but anyway . . . before we keep hopping around all conclusively-like in our own discussion world, I think it is important to just get language out of the way. So let's spill it out . . . how do *you* cling to labels, because I'd like to see **if you know what you're talking about**. I mean—

We have this process of externalizing words, translated from pictorial ideas, and from that one might dichotomize two opposite strains of internal objectives. One strain may absent-mindedly pour out paint can after paint can of colorfully splashing words. Another strain may take the brief moment to find his brush and dip it in the appropriate colors. The man who finds his brush later takes a step back from what he has painted and sees a picture—that of a story— the story of his creation. The other man next to him keeps splashing his buckets of paint cans, on and on, until he notices his supply is running short. He takes a step back, puts his hand to the back of his head, and wonders of what he has become. He sees nothing of what he has created. *Know what you are talking about*, and begin to know the story of your creation.

//Martin pauses with concern that the discussion might just be "running around in circles". Although the implication is not straightforward, "running around in circles" refers to his perception of the state of human existence: Things occur cyclically, coming and going, with no sense of ultimate purpose. The metaphor aims to elicit self-knowledge and heightened awareness of one's thought process, which in turn leads to a special knowledge about the "story" of your creation. "Story" and "creation" contain the further association to a purposeful creative force that began the "story" of our universe. The key to this greater understanding is being carefully attentive to the idea-to-word translation process.//

Peter: I must say, Martin, I enjoy your images. Especially those things you say are "that of a story." The word "story" has brilliant simplicity and associates well within the human mind as a conveniently abstract notion that facilitates thoughts about what is our universe. All other descriptions would cloud holism/comprehensiveness and certainly insert inadequate details. Although certain traits of the universe are easily overlooked as a type of "given" notation, such traits often fit nicely within the frame of what one conceives a story to be: The dynamic feature of such story being the qualities and implications of time continuum – most notably the **one-directional** nature of time. In other words, in a true story there are no rehearsals and no retakes.

WHAT NEXT?

David: It's coming to me: I can see that morality, ethics—you know—the typical splash of society will eventually come up in discussion, and we'll start talking about morals, goals, and ends. I'll say now that I foresee myself about to go off. I'm just warning you.

//David is caught in his own expectations and anticipations. His foresight may be accurate, but his urgency is extreme.//

Martin: No problem, bud. No need to re-strain here.

Jimmy: All this ethics B.S. is nonsense! This is "good," and this is "bad" . . . yeah maybe on some level, but what's the big rush to divide people into opposing camps!? What's the big chase to sort and categorize people!? Why is it necessary? It's so hurried and infantile – it's inherently fake. I say we get to it when He comes?

Prescott: I would have to agree that categorizing is fake, but there is no getting around its everyday use and facilitations. But, you all know, Truth is not everyday or facile. Even as I yearn for understanding, I must always create general categories to make progress. Like once, I understood two types of people: There are those who embrace ethical reasoning in order to feel certain about their goodness and, more importantly, to feel certain about what is "bad," and there are those who take great care to understand the badness they experience so that it might somehow reconcile with the good. Maternal instinct would assume steer you clear of the hurt, as we tend to be taught from the beginning, but I always wondered . . . should the goal of parents be to keep children close to the bosom so that they utterly fear the day of hurt, or should it be our goal to develop solid grounding so that we might venture **alone** *without fear*? I denounce the deliberate categorization that ethics provokes and instead say beware to understand the eternal sadness, for through the tears of the *fallen one* you will find the open heart of the savior – unconditional. Only there.

David: You melt the guilt, my friend.

Prescott: If the devil were not crying, what would Jesus be doing . . . with no one's tears to catch?[1]

//Prescott has pushed everyone into the deep end of the emotional pool. His depth of emotional awareness is stunning. The truth behind ethics is found to be relativistic and unsatisfying. It is of note that the "fallen one" is a devil figure, while the savior figure should go without saying . . . //

Martin: I would say the concept of "Hell" is a copout.

Jimmy: Yeah. They (yeah, they) love the Hitler example, from a high horse:

"So you're saying Hitler is not evil?????" Says they.

---

[1]   We all fall to the pits of anger and ill feeling, and at these points our attention is forced to contemplate the *why* – eternal truths. This understood, I take delight in *sharing a meal with the devil*, as it is quite a lesson. Because to know the Truth, you must know its opposition.

Evil Schmevil. Actually what I'm saying is that you covet his example to feel good about yourself. If any true evil exists, it's your coveting his example to give height to your high horse. I can see that you'd be lost without him.[2]

Prescott: They teach with tones of denunciation, so no wonder their children denounce and discriminate. When their children denounce others, in lack of empathetic openness to include everyone, these new parents do it again and denounce the children of the newest generation, using them as "examples" **not** to follow. So the cycle continues, and new children denounce: They hate your examples, and so they hate.

Peter: They move away out of fear, unknowing; they fear the inability to understand where *I'm* coming from . . . My so called "person" may be attributed to my cause of action or where I am coming from, but the distinction of what is this person is at best unclear. If whatever "I" may be has motivational force and this force is the best definition of "me," then I could be defined by my results; however this fantastic notion of "responsibility" for my self/force and its results is just that – fantastic. Ultimate responsibility is not to any*one* or any*thing*, for responsibility requires some eternal categorization of individuals by some responsibilitizer. Categorization is not real or substantive in telling the intricacies of the storied individual. It is only convenient and natural to the associative networks of the human mind. Responsibility would require a categorizing, responsibilitizing supernatural – a notion not uncommon but utterly ridiculous.

---

[2]   Should silence fall or conversely there is a clash of emotional titans, it is easy to become scared and run back home where they call it "evil." Evil will exist as long as we call its name. The sickest part is that when we perceive its presence, we desire a face for association and condemnation.

//Ethics and the categorization of individuals, especially the contaminated desire to call someone "evil," is agreed to be one of the most terribly backwards and widely-accepted habits of humanity. Humanity is seen to have invented the concept of "Hell" as a way to banish from sight those things that are most difficult to understand.//

Jimmy: Ethics [laugh]. . . shit ain't real. As long as you don't contradict yourself, you're right. What kinda shit is that? They have no ultimate point. . .

Oh wow, I just realized that I have no point. No point. NONE. None whatsoever. I get to no point when there was a point if there ever was a point. when where and how. I have no point.

David: I told you we should get to the point.

//Again, they speak of a "point": A moment or state that signifies completion.//

Martin: So what's the point of the story? If there were no story, could there be any moral? In other words, if humanity as one storied whole had no universally/supernaturally delegated goal, could there be any moral to extract from our existence? **No**, no there wouldn't – there would be no point. I should be able to stab you in the face with a six inch blade, swirl the blade around in your skull until I amassed a nice chuck of flesh and brain, and then eat your flesh straight off the knife. Then I might dig out the remainder of your flesh and brain, put it in a blender, and comfortably gulp down your gooey flesh. Would this be wrong?? Are you disgusted by my words, what possessed me? Did you feel my words?? If humanity is not somehow supernaturally bound by a universal goal, how can my hypothetical feast somehow be "immoral" or, as I would say, against the moral of the story? It couldn't be – because there's no point. So I stop to ask: what is *our* goal? Shouldn't we have one? Shouldn't we agree on it – at first?

Peter: A goal implicates direction. Only though **one** said committed direction can *we* say there exists misdirection, that is, being "misdirected" away from what is to be learned from following the one true direction. Agreed that this unsaid something that is supposed to be learned might be best understood through the concept of "moral," or the moral of the story. Having a moral eludes unto a goal; therefore a universal goal must be present to designate a moral. Perceived moral standards of society should not hold the subjected masses choked before universality is accepted genuinely and direction is made clear. Early and modern moral codes are unclear in direction but appealing to the immediate and narrow directions of daily conscious life, only to stave off uncertainty. Its stranglehold is devious.

//Martin's purposely disgusting scenario (as to stir emotional attention) is analytically complemented by Peter. His notion of direction could be taken to mean different things, but it generally speaks among a fairly specific class of ideas: "Direction" is best defined in this instance as a state of being that involves communal attention to the learning of a greater Truth. It is important to note the communal aspect of this attention: Peter exclaims that individuals cannot be forced into communal attention regarding their path of existence until communal "direction is made clear."//

David: First, let me state Our goal: Our goal is Truth. Every single number, every single word, and every single action we put forth somehow resembles—resembling in resemblance—Our One goal, which is Truth. *Luckily*, Truth happens to be Love, Truth happens to be the Spirit, Truth happens to be . . . One: something of no numerical value.

What you define as gravity, I see as a physical representation of the Spirit – the One true force that brings us All together. What you define as the Big Bang, I see as a physical representation of Oneness broken, or the beginning of multiple things—ouch—breaking, separation to Our world – multiple eyes, multiple people.

Everything in Our world is numerical: We could count every particle in our universe one-by-one if we had the time, and I am sure we would if we did because the practice is all too common: Through these numbers we have found great power. I add up my muscle power, I add up my "intelligence," I add up my speed, my allies, my everything. We do these things in order to say what is best because it is the only way we know how . . . This is Our flaw: We use numbers as power when Our true nature is One. The Spirit, however, is readily present in *all* of Our numbers: We all understand the persecution of being alone versus the power of being united. We yearn to share our beliefs so that Our certainty about life is strong. America is the haven of this certainty: We are free to share our beliefs without persecution, so our strength is immense. But you all are my brothers and sisters – We do everything toward the same end . . . I . . . do these numbers mean that much to you? Perhaps they do, but there exists something greater: Something of no numerical value that cannot choose sides. This is the Spirit. This is Love. This is Us when We were One. This is what We can share. I can't count or enumerate to you how this all works out because I don't count anymore – I share, and I combine. Why is 3 a holy number? A 3rd force between me and you? Well, don't listen to a word I say . . . do you *feel* what I say in word? It is okay to doubt: With the strength of the Spirit you will find all your doubts, and with the strength of all your doubts you will find the Spirit . . . thoughts cancel.

//David's splurge expresses a genuine fascination with nature's symbolism. Citing specific examples (Gravity & Big Bang), he illustrates a deeper, divinely symbolic meaning behind the workings of the universe: He associates observed phenomena with the nature of a divine force (The Spirit), which is to say that the nature of "God" is expressed symbolically throughout the universe. David moves with his symbolism to state mystically his conception of the universe as a functioning, singular whole. He remarks on the "numerical" state of things, i.e., there are multiple parts to the whole (following the Big Bang). His observations are interesting to the others, but his quickly assembled abstraction of the universe leaves many details not discussed . . . //

Jimmy: And I thought *I* should slow down . . . wow partner, your abstraction is not of this world.

Prescott: How we yearn to attain things not of this world...If you want to bring the sky to the ground, you must be prepared to leave the ground, maybe forever. Are you prepared to give it all up? As Jesus said, you must hate your life in order to be His disciple. Not necessarily your "life" in literal terms, but the **certainty**[3] of life you have found by burying yourself in earthly manners and matters. Jesus' message is truly not of *this* world.

---

[3] Certainty is the rewarding affirmation that promotes the settlement of a point of view. False or earthly certainties most often involve professional or economic management until one becomes *satisfied* and *situated* in some stable routine that aptly re-nourishes the basic human needs—daily deeds. These deeds may become the ultimate representation of one's self-standing and in turn how one derives their self-worth. It is the simple pride of some unwavering fixture, with economic reliability often being the ultimate criteria of that fixture. It then becomes one's ultimate aim and reward, diverting oneself from the newfounds of mental growth. It might be seen that some professions tend to divert more than others.

David: I can relate to you Prescott . . . your word "certainty." There is nothing certain about humanity and its propositions: humankind has not established a universal goal. We are imperfect, so as primitive beings We were not able to communicate well enough to establish universal common ground. It's not readily apparent **why** We exist, so humankind has proceeded to define all physical realities and relationships in terms and objectives that are personal to the describer(s) of the time, leaving us now with only limited space for association. This is a learning process or "childhood" which helps Us define the things around us and those things' relation to us, further developing our identity as a self-reflective species. It is this learning process that sets us apart from all other animals. I attest, then, that Our process of defining things has no need to continue. For if We have completely gone through the process of defining the things around us, We may then see the pattern in humanity that may lead us to a greater truth of existence. Our numerical definitions will never explain the power behind Our existence, so in Our quest toward Truth We must stop defining the things around us and begin exploring why these definitions and laws were *made* the way they were. If we can now learn from the things happening around us, we might find that a universal Human goal is based in Truth and Love. If this could happen, I have a feeling that the Truth found would free Us all from Our troubles and differences. There We could communicate with a backbone and understand Our lives' troubles. We are children here on earth. Children learn from their lives of rules and judgment in order to find something greater . . .

//The comforting intentions of Prescott are finding success in David, allowing him to achieve some temporary degree of relaxation about his thoughts. His present words about universal purpose are somewhat more clear and precise than usual. He plants and cultivates the notion that the "earthly life" of humanity is in a sense like "childhood". "Childhood," in his words, is a process of learning from rules and limitations. The rules and limitations of language are the focus of humanity's goal, according to David. He makes it clear that these rules are supernaturally embedded and motivated by some ultimate purpose; therefore, we should reflect on the intentions behind these constraints in order to discover a greater Truth.//

Jimmy: What could be greater than a never ending childhood? If you all think you're "grown up," you can kiss my ass cuz I'm not goin nowhere. No, sorry, you are all decent . . . but you're still old. Alright, alright, I'll share this one with you I wrote last week because it's good timing:

Never Ending Childhood:

I was always thinking to myself, "Where the hell am I going right now? What the hell is this place?" I stopped thinking like a robotic **word** machine and answered the question with the true part of my brain; I was dreaming. I asked the same question to the people who write the laws, and they were frightened by me. They looked at me like I had come back from the dead – a sort of zombie's revenge.

I did come back from the dead.
They had killed me long ago
When I didn't know any better.
I was a baby boy when I didn't understand the things around me.
Every
Time
I'd say "What is this place?"
The law writers would speak words and give names.
I was weak and confused, so I believed what they said.
I've gone through all of their schools now
So I think I'm smart enough to ask why:

Why they put a brick in my mind like that
Without telling me . . .
I got no answer.
They just called me names;
They called me crazy.
Hmm.
I guess when you try and label the un-labelable,
You call *me* crazy.
This is Our world . . .
I can't label it.
I just think it's crazy.
Crazy enough to have a lot of fun with . . .
If we wanted?
So where did all the fun go?
Into the brick I say:
Growing up is for chumps.
I know *my* bed time.
I think I like right nowzzzzzzzzzzzzzzzzzzzzzzzz
asdfd aasd awdf asdfasd
Oh, good morning!
It's so good to see you again!

Prescott: Good to see you too!

Jimmy: Lemme share one more quick one . . . it's on point:

I hated sentences
for the shortest time

Wow, that was the longest time of my life. I guess all I had to do
is realize how manufactured they are. Sentences. When I realized
how manufactured they are, I realized something real that I never
wrote was real before. I felt it was real. So sure, I'll join the sentence
assembly line with you.

Peter: Yeah, those pesky sentence models that are recalled to sound fitting.

//Jimmy feels corrupted and unduly limited by society's impositions. In observing his thoughts he understands that gradual idea formations do not necessarily occur in grammatical order. Grammatical correctness and other strict regimentations of expression are thus the subject of Jimmy's denunciation: The strict order of sentences, paragraphs, and so forth places limits on the expression and clarity of mental constructs, much to the contempt of Jimmy. He is learning to move past this with the help and recognition of the others.//

Turning Around

David: It's funny: the Christian overtones of our discussion have been allowing us to share modes of thought. This one in particular I will have to agree with – the holiness of childhood . . . Children, wandering by virtue of their ignorance, seem to hint at the most existentially pertinent of questions. "Adults" will speak of Truth and say, "F=ma." Children will then ask, "*why* does F=ma?" Adults develop simple minded lessons with certainty: "don't do bad things, or bad things will happen. (ifâthen)" Children remain curiously frustrated: "Why do bad things happen if I do these things? (if this, *why* that or anything?)" There is an equation here with two sides. And without both sides, the story could not be told in full. We are part of a story where We all need each other to have definition. Reason guides our choices, but in the ultimate moment my reason holds against choosing sides – the way of the child.

Prescott: The will of a child speaks but one word: PLAY! Play, young one, while the sun is out. On the one hand, there is difference between you and me; on the other hand, there is a lifetime of similarity. I have seen us play here on the ground, by and through many ways and wills. I have begun at last to see inside the packages that deliver the images of our soul. And yes, we do differ. With our thoughts and actions we *all* offer unique answers to the basic questions of identity: What are your toys? What are your games? Perhaps questions never to be answered in a word...that is unless you follow the rule and lost the game.

Jimmy: I'm sorry to interrupt all the warm feelings, but if we are limited, if our movement depends on rules, if our progression relies on reactions, if these reactions abide by rules, if we must conserve our momentum, if force has proportionate counterparts . . . if we are subject to **rules**, these rules must represent some higher intelligence, you know . . . it's just like parents . . . they can't let you go out on your own. They have to lay down some *ground* rules first. They're keeping our feet on the ground. I understand that now. So when is the barrier gonna be lifted? I think we need to go back to school – back to our playground.

Martin: When I was a young boy, I cried myself to sleep. I had in my head the imagination-come-real of a never-ending circle or swirl-type-dealy, and I would retrace it over and over until I could feel the presence of eternal time. It scared the Be-Jesus out of me, so I cried and screamed out something like, "Forever is so scary!! But I don't want to die!"

Earthly life is our childhood, a sweet story infused with enough pain to feel, along with a definitive ending. Our story ends . . . but we don't . . .

David: Yeah, but is my entire life part of a pre-destined story?? They say, you know, that that doesn't seem right . . . who likes the idea that we can't choose our own destiny? Would we be free if we could not choose our own destiny?? Ha, they wish they were free. I see destiny written all over this world. Through every word and every number I see this process eventually coming to an end, and part of me doesn't like it. I see destiny written all over my life, and that same part of me doesn't like it. But this is only my childhood . . . here I can appreciate a story with a truthful ending. A child doesn't want to hear a long story with no ending!

Peter: Heh Heh. I was always fascinated with this particular tendency of children—to the effect of: "Read me a story—one with a happy ending—and I will fall fast asleep."

Jimmy: It's like . . . give me something *complete*, and I can let everything go, losing consciousness, knowing that there is no guarantee that I will awaken.

//David recognizes the pervasiveness of "Christian overtones" in the discussion, emphasizing "holiness of childhood" as an essential thread of the discussion. Children and childhood are subject to expansive discussion: They all work around the idea that humanity's existence is a type of "childhood." Prescott makes the appealing proposition that as children on earth our identities can be defined by our personal "toys" and "games." This leaves room for the listener to imagine for him or herself what these toys and games might represent. Essentially, Prescott is referring to personalized processes of playful thought and various forms of self-entertainment. The list of what could be considered someone's "game" is endless (which is Prescott's intention). Martin responds with a story from his younger years, describing a mental limbo between the fear of death and the fear of no end (immortality), which is further developed by David: He conceives that humanity's divinely true story will provide resolution to the fear of no end, while eternal life awaits the end of the story, conjunctively resolving the fear of death and the fear of no end. Peter then gives a very pertinent example of a childhood tendency. It implies that there is a primeval human desire for a sense of completion, such as a story might produce.//

Prescott: The existence of sleep, as a necessity, embodies human suffering: The mind becomes so chained and bogged down in the layers of living that it eventually ceases and virtually breaks from the body, as if it were no longer able to carry on this charade.

[*Yawns*][4]

Jimmy: I noticed you brought up destiny, Dave, and I am wondering why no one has brought up the concept of "free will." I think it's some bullshit myself – probably the biggest illusion suffered by most all of humanity. I mean, "free?" What the hell does that mean? Everything has some type of limit or natural inclination imposed on it. "Free?" Oh, okay, freeeeeee . . . I'm floating, weeee, weeee. What a joke. All I know is I'm stuck to the ground.

Martin: If God is *both* beginning and end, his *destination* must be *pre*.

Jimmy: Ha, nice one. True.

David: What I get a lot of is this: "Well, I believe I *do* have free will, and that I *can* make choices. I can either go get in my car or go to the bathroom." Yes, maybe you could see yourself doing one thing or another at any given moment, but a gradual realization must still be made. Before any thought begins, before any movement ventures through space, before any time is pierced, there will first be some micro-goal to trigger its happensake – some end motivation through which it has a capacity to venture, experience, express, etc. Did you ever try and just STOP? Nothing more, just stop? I get the urge to achieve total absence often, especially lying in bed with songs of the day re-playing and penetrating my mental forces. So I see it really is impossible to stop. Something is always in line—next—to run

---

4   Everyone yawned at once. As they stepped into each others' shoes, they wondered: Who yawned first?

through my head. It can be a pretty relentless parade, and sometimes I wish it didn't, but it does: It owns me – my way to go. Always go.[5]

Peter: In the meticulous order of processes, where each microcosmic jump, so to speak, from axon to dendrite and all in between, is of teleological nature (that of purposefully following some primeval force in its perpetuation), there will be summated a perfect series of events, with a pattern of progression that becomes of self-transcendent meaning to any intelligent observer subject therein. Any such observers would reside of meaningful measurement between the micro and macro, as the human being may reflect on being stuck pitifully between the two . . .[6]

The capacity to "make choices" is an illusory perception: It is a *dual perception of potential* (not dual power). Nothing is "free." Freedom, in the fantastic sense we love to use it, is not real. It is meaningless to merely say that "I am free": To use the word realistically it must be in reference to some capacity, for everything is subject to limitations and the impositions of nature. Humans do not choose their capacities and frameworks; they are *imposed* on us as something we're forced to work with . . .

If I have a "will" and that will must "stop & choose," then my unchanging will should already be determined in its intrinsic protocol. Or if my will in some way can "change in choosing", then what is it that wills that change in my will? It seems that if my will can change, then what changes my will is actually my true will. And maybe there should be another change in will before the choice, and

---

5   Fate is never, until. Its clarity is never, until retrospect. The gradual forward has no sight to stop.

6   For all shifts in organizational energy—zoomed to the microstages—so called motivations of local shift, there must be a transcendent "Father Principle" through which all shifts have a meaningful, interconnected direction outside the locale.

another change, and so on such that the room for change in will is a mysterious one, and I am locked out again – outside the will of change. I may concede that humans make "choices" for the sake of argument, but "freedom" about these choices is still merely an example of incorrect imagination.[7]

Jimmy: It's funny I was thinking, my freedom lies solely in my stupidity. There are so many things going on inside my body. So many actions and reactions. Trillions of cells each doing their own preordained little duty. I don't check the departure time of all these flights . . . you know about like being along for the ride . . . that's not my shit, but you know, I am so stupid, I am so ignorant, that I have no sight to see my objective as a unit soul. It feels great, I guess. I feel as smooth as flight:

Swiftly walking here and there.
Swiftly talking – observe and share.

I might try and sit down for a moment to try and trick myself. Maybe I can quickly do something that I wasn't meant to do – a little "instachange." At the edge of the moment in time I might think it's possible, but I am always left hanging on the edge, and then it's done with, and I see that I changed nothing at all. I will always have a reason to do what I do. It's the ignorance that keeps me in the flow and makes me feel free. I just thought it was funny, I was thinking.

//It becomes emphatic that free will is an illusion.//

---

[7] The term "incorrect imagination" arose quite naturally, thanks to a conversation between good friends about this hypothetical tree supposedly falling in the woods. One perspective of the thought experiment required imagining oneself not existing, which was quickly objected to and termed an incorrect imagination. A very true oxymoron.

David: I'm going to say what is going through my head now. Okay? I'm trying to stay with you . . .

I am here in my childhood, and I see the course of America as one with no end – no goal. Democracy assumes we will be divided for all eternity, and I don't think this is true. God bless America, and God bless the time when we move on to something greater. Democracy appears to have a goal. Did we not have a goal in mind? Of course we did. Let us discuss it. Let me think first.

Jimmy: I get frustrated too when I start talking politics. It's just not for me, you know . . . what's the point if there will be no eternal human government?

Martin: As a man, I loved political philosophy. Such a noble and spirited pursuit it was. My growth projected deep into this field at a time; it was a giant step that I leaped atop – a step unavoidable. Things have changed. I am a Child now. The long, fantastic tale of Polly M. Sci now only taunts my ambition, for this story has no end. I am a Child now. My story will have an end.

David: Okay, I have seen, and I have thought, and I am not so sure that we really want to reach this goal. A successful democracy results in the complete *personalization* of priorities and morals. Hello America, how perfect you are—perfect in execution—but personalization is both the positive label you might imagine, and a potential prison to all mankind. This personalization is in full effect, so it now becomes Our only goal to divide and protect these personal playpens. If the Spirit of Truth did not drive us into communities, I would disintegrate in fear upon gazing at America: A communal goal is non-existent. What happens when existential crises arise? What happens when we discuss Our (how ironic) "communal" issues? We blabber and we taunt – we distinguish on majority and corruption. We distinguish this way, and we flush one another down the shoot.

Our success will flush everyone down eventually, and a new time will come.

Prescott: When you are tired, you can never be yourself. If you can never be yourself, you will always be tired. So I am forced to go to sleep – everyday. Until the true day that never *falls* asleep. You have been awake for "success" too long now, America. I wish I could show you how tired you are. We are sleepless in America – faceless in America. Please, come rest with me.

Jimmy: We sleep everyday. Why? I could never say for sure, but I'm guessing that we all just get damn tired of putting on a show.

Prescott: If there is anything I know, it is that the secret is in your dreams. It is here we have a chance to be ourselves. *This* is Our goal – simply to be ourselves. This I swear to you from the deepest thrones of my heart – *be yourself.* There you will find the Spirit: you will find the Truth. *This* Truth will set you free. Sweet dreams . . . *when you wake*, it will make all the sense in the world.

//David and Jimmy make the important point that no political order will reign forever. David then takes his frustration and expresses it outward, resulting in a negative depiction of the objectives of American Democracy. David and Prescott both create the image of America as "tired". Prescott reveals the backbone of his teachings, telling all to "be yourself," for in the "tired" state of America it is our *true* selves that are put to sleep: He depicts the "tired" state as a perilous cycle of self-presentation: Mis-transforming your true person produces tiredness, and tiredness produces a mis-transformation of your true person.//

Martin: I like that Prescott. "Be Yourself": Simple yet infinitely deep.

Jimmy: So do you tell yourself who you are, or just are you? Can we be without telling ourselves to be? I don't think so, but which one comes first?? Back and forth I go: Life becomes a fluctuation between being, evaluating/reflecting on that being, and moving with that evaluation of being to a new being – by and through telling myself what be me and what next to be, only to again be onward to another reevaluation and a new telling to be. That was a long sentence, so again, I ask: where did I begin? what came first?

Peter: Yes, let's talk about knowledge of self:

As social beings, we find ourselves saddled with an externally oriented awareness. This awareness may come and go, having peaks and valleys of orientation throughout the day, depending on the social impositions of our changing lively circumstances. It is easy to ignore the dragging force that places your self-presence as sustained and intertwined with the external world. It is, in a sense, an unconscious and unrelenting push that gives one the assurance that *We are all in this together*, as We are part of something greater—a communal whole—a **Grand Consciousness.**[8] Togetherness has a nice ring, but I have found that we sacrifice the expression of our true selves in order to maintain the comfortability [yes, "comfortability" is a word that enjoys the versatility of childlike conjugations] of the Grand Consciousness. This maintenance of comfortabilty is a type of blind optimism or haven of superficial certainty. The expense of this haven may be knowledge of true self:

To break from the external world, social customs, habits of interactions, expectations *to follow*, falling in line, etc., is to question the essence of your own certainty and also the certainty of the

---

8   Although the overlay of the Grand Consciousness is unique to each individual in terms of how it gives texture to one's external world experiences, this layer of attention is nevertheless collective and essentially identical in its permeation throughout humanity.

Grand Consciousness. By questioning the certainty of the Grand Consciousness in more personal mental recesses we can develop new reasoned understandings of how selves function internally and how selves go **so far** (and, wow, sometimes it is very far) in order to orient oneself with the external. Going-so-far-as-to-relate is a type of external scrutiny (as one must traverse a substantial mental distance and thereby have the time and opportunity to recognize the terrain and obstacles through which one must travel to meet the external) and becomes crucial to understanding the self:

To recede from the external is to develop a more evolved understanding of one's actual relation with the external, for if one stays attached to the certain appeal of the Grand Consciousness, one may never separate and find one's true self. In more words: The Grand Consciousness relies on smooth skin and happy trails. Its objective is not to comprehend the unipoint (origin), or nexus, of all paths, but to keep the surface smooth and avoid the unknown/uncomfortable. To fall to the appeal of the peachy Grand Consciousness, like an external vacation, is to avoid the internal that is one's true self, resulting in a kind of arrested development of the true self. It is an attractive danger to fall into permanent vacation, for if one is then directed back inward somehow, they will surely turn away in fear, leaving their true selves **alone**. Many true selves are left weeping, alone.

[*A pause signifies that everyone can relate – to the core.*]

Prescott: Truly honest relationships reveal new truths about yourself. Given this, imagine all humankind openly sharing all their traits, all their worries, and everything that binds humanity. Only by the Spirit of Love may we join. Only there do we see Truth of being: Truth is Everyone – in One.

Because of Our emotional and logical caprice, Our nature is clouded. Our certainty behind life's path is nowhere to be found, and Our conclusions are tethered to superficial directions – Our goal is out of sight. There is a **Great Uncertainty** about humanity's relationship with the external world that either becomes individually repressed or confronted. A greater uncertainty does not exist, so then Our lives, in full, are governed by this link of uncertainty that binds humanity, for it is everything we can do to divert from awareness and suffocate this uncertainty. It is everything we can be to find our way. Take a look around, I beg you: What are *you* doing right now? What am *I* doing right now? We may not have met, but I know you. I swear I do.

As the universality of human goals becomes more ambiguous, the search for meaning behind these goals becomes pointless, without a point. How may we discuss details (government, morality, drugs, war) without starting from a non-relative foundation? We certainly give our lives trying, but it is no coincidence that Our discussions are forever unfinished – Our goal is still hidden. Money, fame (self-worth), politics, and so on have replaced the sense of One communal goal with countless numbers of personal goals. This mindset fuels us all as animals, but divides us all as humans. We are thus in a constant struggle to bind with one another – to assure one another that the Spirit of Love truly connects us all:

"I feel for you."
"I am happy for you."
"I know what you mean."
"I Love you."

So be it then our eternal search for Truth. Seeking and searching everyday as time speeds up, slows down, and stands still. All confined to our safe-haven minds, our heads are locked tight from persecution to a point of seclusion and division where talking with yourself becomes the only honest back-and-forth flow of Spirit........................
Holy Jesus! We are only human! We cannot progress alone! Who now will reach down and embrace Our loving thoughts which we

know to be true? Forever stuck within ourselves and our faith alone, who now will share this with me? Who will assure that my Love is good? This loneliness and uncertainty I cannot take: It is the burden of all mankind. It lives in Everything as humanity struggles to unify.

Q: The safety and freedom of being alone is infinitely precious, for here there is potential for total and complete honesty. Now, out into the world we go, yearning for the same loving company that was our self. "What will they think of me?" I don't know . . . so I wonder how can we save our personal freedom from corruption, while still coming together as a community?

A: As people judge one another, humankind is torn apart, and the beautiful Truth of our existence is withheld in fear. Only by the Spirit of Love does the fear and uncertainty end. I say then that it is the goal of all mankind to end our judging ways—to combine personal and communal freedom into the Spirit that binds us all into One living life force—One undying truce. We must reconcile our differences, as I Love you All and Everything you have to share with me. Here We find Truth. Here We Live

//Prescott outlines a goal for humanity. He then states a fundamental truth that serves as the foundation of his outline: Self-knowledge is gained in community. In other words, the people around you allow comparative two-way reflection and therefore self-definition. The "Great Uncertainty" is an integral concept that defines the lonely, uncertain nature of human being: As a single person, there is no mode of internal confirmation, that is, to gain certainty we require the presence of others. Humanity, in complete unification, becomes the source and embodiment of Truth and certainty – infinite confirmation. Prescott acknowledges the obstacles to this unification. Simply put, they are the prevailing preference of *personal* goals (as opposed to a single communal goal) and the insecure, judging nature of humans. An important distinction is made between personal and social worlds (mental worlds that is): He expresses the sanctity of personal thought as having a greater potential to be uninhibited and free in its expressions. Social thought, on the other hand, immediately creates a sense of inhibition about expressions.[9] His solution, therefore, is to develop social atmospheres with the same freedom that lay within personal thought.//

David: A paparratzi. How in the world do you spell poparatzi? Anyway. This is the judger of everything you do. It follows you everywhere as an invisible cage is placed around you. You have no freedom. As we judge one another, our freedom to follow the Spirit is lost. Our world is made up of numbers – numbers which have their result in the form of all judgments: If we were One, would we judge our self?? I tell you there was a time when we were One, and Our unified nature was that of Truth. It was here that we were free. Can you have faith in something that lacks numerical value? Don't judge me, and this is possible.

Jimmy: I once said to a teacher, "I don't believe in judging because . . . well, I don't think it's smart." He replied with a twisted eyebrow, "Well, isn't it our duty to judge?" That was basically the extent of the conversation, but I would have liked to have given an open response:

It is not our 'duty' to judge, but our mighty ambition in a world of labels and improper distinctions. When you find the Spirit, your last "earthly" choice is made: Will I judge? Or will I Love? What a supremely ironic "last choice": to choose correctly is to not choose [sides] – to not judge. It will often be the voices of utilitarianism battling the Spirit – a devilishly lopsided match. Utilitarianism will have everything on its side: home turf, words/labels, and especially

---

9   Life is the process of gaining an audience, followed by the frustration of realizing that there is more than one.

numbers. It will be powerful and focused, utilizing its intrinsically one dimensional captivations.

//David's paparazzi example describes a fundamental social obstacle to the openness of expression in community: There are social expectations of behavior that act as a type of normalizing force, filtering the uniqueness of an individual's truth of expression. With a biblical mindset, Jimmy moves along to develop an image of the so called "Judgment Day." He debunks traditional conceptions of this divine event that speak of a time when "God" judges the living and the dead. His focus on the action of "judgment" involves a communal choice (or lack thereof) for all of humanity: will **we** include everyone? – will **we** judge or love? In other words, will **our** heart be vengeful or open. He uses the communal pronoun in reference to humanity, proclaiming that every single person is a necessary piece of Truth. He implements an image of Our universe's primordial state of singularity (Oneness), which is described as having a motivational nature of Truth at the exclusion of no one.//

Peter: One-dimensional thought: Looks forward to no ultimate goal and proceeds course on a superficially brilliant philosophy: immediate satisfaction. There becomes a one-sided fear where earthly suffering is the outcome that is to be avoided. In the unstoppable continuum of time, the pursuit of pleasure and migration from pain eventually leaves us at the hands of death with nothing to say. The final stop on earth arrives, and the sense of attention to earthly sufferings becomes twisted: There is a diminishing motivation to anticipate the future (foresight distance) because death blocks all foresight upon confrontation. There is nothing to look forward to.[10]

---

[10] He looks forward to nothing and sees everything.

Martin: And it is the things we look forward to that keep us moving through the day: A paycheck, a playground recess, a shot, a joint, a break. It is a grim thought to understand that this continuum leads to death. The trip is just too one-way. However, if our goal is to experience, and not necessarily to prevent pain, our trip about earth may reach new dimensions. The only problem is this innate fear of death, apparently leaving us nothing to look forward to. Have no fear. There is much more than we see here.

Prescott: Our sufferings are defined on the surface of the earth:

Sure, I don't want to "mess up my life" . . . I am so uncertain of my path that I certainly should not destroy the one mapped out for me by the grains of society. We were so uncertain with our existence that our ancestors buried the thought of uncertainty: Here, on the ground, we have certainties that were defined for us by our ancestors. We have formed America: A country so certain of itself that it feels like wonderland. What a remarkable achievement! We have destroyed the Great Uncertainty – the cause of all grief! What crazy man would want to leave this place?? John Lennon, Dr. King . . . .Jesus? These were the seekers of Truth rather than certainty. Please don't kill me too. Please define success before you mark my path to it.

As long as the sufferings we share and discuss are confined to the surface we walk on, we will find nothing greater than the surface we walk on, as our discussions of Truth resemble a dog-fight, confined to the nature of animals.

//Martin dwells on the fact that humans are motivated by their expectations and anticipations and that we live solely to rendezvous with them. Also, there is an innate survival mechanism that senses and steers clear of pain, placing a limit on what we might wish to experience. At first glance Martin sees the foresight of one's eventual extermination as truthfully far-sighted (in that death **is** eventual), while the seeking of pleasure is ignorantly nearsighted in that there is no eternal satisfaction. He sees humanity as nearsighted because of the fear and repression of the inevitability of death. Prescott elaborates on this thought, exclaiming that our fear of straying from society's **safe** path to wealth and happiness leaves us nearsighted to superficial ("on the surface"), earthly pleasures. Prescott notes that this is appealing to humans because it is an immediate and readily available source of certainty; this immediate certainty is, however, only temporary and feeds no Truth to the soul. The avoidance of innate human uncertainty, or identity confusion if you will, places limits on our minds' freedom to venture, keeps us obliviously nearsighted, and shackles us in concern of only earthly satisfactions.//

Jimmy: It is a difficult task to say what a human is like in his "natural" state. When I say "natural man", I don't wish to tell you how a man acts in some defined "natural state"—whether protective or aggressive, sage-like or peace-like—all that crap they've said before. Rather, I mean to present a hypothetical scenario, left to your *own* imagination. It is only proper:

Imagine a full-grown man (or woman) instantly created and placed somewhere alone on earth. He has no knowledge of what anything might be named or called. He is completely speechless of his surroundings. And more importantly, his form of note taking (memory) has just begun. This is natural man – unsubject to the blasphemy that his brothers and sisters, mothers and fathers might have possibly created.

What [in the world] would go through this man's head? I'm sure he would have some excellent questions . . . if he could only speak! How ironic. From here, the theory of human ignorance evolves: There are three questions that natural man is sprung to answer:

Who am I?
Where am I? And
Why am I here?

I always wondered why we skip over basic questions. Where in the world did these questions go?! Why do we skip and refuse to pose them? It is either the fear of our own ignorance, or it is that we are so focused, so enslaved by our tasks and judgments at hand, that the road of attention to these questions is naturally detoured. I believe these two factors play into one:

We are raised as children to focus on the task at hand: A child may ask, "What is that, daddy?" At which point the father might not explain the existence of the object in question; instead he might simply give the object a name in order to make the child assured and certain of his surroundings. Essentially we tell our children to "shut your traps," "don't ask that question again," and "when that question creeps into your head again, just retrieve the labels I have taught you, and this will satisfy your ignorance."

I will ask the question again, "Where am I?" And still the breeded mind will answer me, "Earth! You fool, earth!" I wish they knew what a silly answer that is. I can label something anyway I wish. I don't use that outhouse anymore. They probably won't answer my question again; they'll just call me crazy. I guess their knowledge works on a whole different system. This system is the focus of our adult life. The child has been all but destroyed, so in posing the three basic questions at this point, we will encounter a point of refusal. The "smartest" people in the world cannot answer the most basic and **ever-probing** three questions of life, yet they awe us with stirring conclusions. It is in this lop-sided world, where the fear of the destruction of our pride (not necessarily best called the fear of our own ignorance) causes us to stay focused and far away from the three questions. After all, we exist . . . yet we walk around as if we created ourselves . . .

[*Thoughts*]

Here's one:

A Man is born in the middle of nowhere
We'll call this place earth.

Man gets hungry,
Man gets tired.

And above all,
Man wants to fuck.
And above *All*,
Man wants to Love

Who knows how he'll do in school tomorrow?

//Jimmy develops a concept of "natural man." After first considering the thoughts of political philosophers ("all that crap **they**'ve said before"), he sees them to be irrelevant in any discussion of eternal Truth. His side of the story creates a hypothetical scenario that is fit only for one's imagination: Clearly this "natural man" could never actually exist, but it is still possible to have a powerful experience when one puts himself in the shoes of this "natural man." Jimmy's objective is to induce this experience and have the listener feel the "natural" ignorance and uncertainty about human existence that natural man is consumed by. He makes another step and imagines three questions that this "natural" ignorance would be prime to ask. They are essentially questions of identity, setting, and purpose; however, each question leads to the other as woven into one. Jimmy proceeds to vent his frustration about the close-minded "focus" of adults. He uses sentiments already discussed to show how children are unintentionally corrupted by their parents: Parents push aside the uncertainty about existence embedded within the child and focus him/her on the superficial developments needed to succeed in society without offering deeper explanations. Jimmy seems to focus much of his contempt on the functioning of school systems: He goes on to use the "natural man" image in a poem, expressing the man's (who was born in the middle of nowhere) primal drives and ending with a stimulating question ("Who knows how he'll do in school tomorrow?"). I.e. natural man was not expecting such external influences . . . so is he ready to receive them?//

Prescott: 21st Century daily life cannot define who we are. We let it. It is only when we come home and discuss the tribulations of these days that we find out who we are.

No one forces us to share our thoughts, our days, but we do so, we need so to live: MIND

No one forces us to get a job, but we do so, we need so to live: BODY

It's *All* in your mind. Don't deny where you live.

Jimmy: So then, what is important on your deathbed, your mental health or your bodily health? Funny question, huh? You might find out that God is not as far away as you think he is—you might find—he is as far away as you *think*.

//Prescott stays somewhat attentive to Jimmy's thoughts about the corruptive effect of society, but he remains with his open mindset about earthly suffering. After saying that "daily life" (which would include school in the eyes of Jimmy) does not define who we are, Prescott focuses importance on one's mental state in regard to identity/truth, rather than the common focus on bodily satisfactions. In conclusion, he preaches that it is most important to know God in mind. Many envision God as far away, on high, and superior, and so then they are obedient. On the contrary, Prescott implicates that God is not superior but everywhere. We must eliminate our fearful subordination in order to truly become aware of the nature of God and ourselves as One. These newfound appropriate behaviors (although "appropriate" would be a dubious word in this discussion) will naturally follow this awareness.//

Jimmy: There is certainly a common power that keeps us all in awe. There is, however, that one moment, or maybe even several scattered moments, when you think, you feel, you know that you really shouldn't be in awe. Then a loud noise sounds – that moment is over. You *remember* what you have been told. Rules stacked on top of rules tear your consciousness to the path of dumbing physicality. I'm working on it though. I know the awe is wrong, and the feeling is right.

I get the feeling, but then it hurts even more to stumble around as a child when everyone has left the playground. Everybody has grown up now, so what am I to do? I know everybody is staring at something? – it seems ok; I just can't keep that focus. I'm too busy staring all around me.

//Jimmy speaks of a "common power that keeps us all in awe" which is actually a somewhat random reference to Thomas Hobbes' Leviathan. This shows his working memory is still focused on thoughts about "natural man." His conception of a "common power" is fairly abstract: Basically "common power" is a combination of rules, impositions, and expectations of society that keep us tentative and self-deprecating.//

David: I guess you could say I am in awe too – in awe of the finite. And soon enough I will understand the rules set into action. I see already their divine symbolism. And once you understand the rules, without truthifying the earthly objectives of words, you will be ready for true adulthood – ready for the infinite . . .

Peter: Whether falsely dilated or not, apocalyptic thought—to the infinite—keens the curious young student within.

Martin: Well, at least you recognize possible false dilation. Hmm . . . [*Thoughts*]. . . Ha. You all tell me what you think about this one:

As man embarks upon the wonders of reason and technology, he is faced with the beginning of a long journey: The river ahead is swift and winding. All of its tributaries are a mystery in terms of quantity and destination. Man ponders and drools over his potential: "I have it! I think we could make a ship so advanced and so flexible in its capabilities, that no matter where the river goes, we will stay afloat. What an accomplishment that would be!" Yeah well, that's great, but don't we want to think about where we're trying to go or even what it looks like? Please wait. Can we at least stop at a rest area to discuss this? Anything? Hmm. . . . I guess they weren't listening.

Jimmy: Say that again – I wasn't listening.

Martin: Ha.

//David again refers to divine symbolism. His ambition pushes his foresight to imagine the end state of humanity, that of pushing past rules and arriving at a place of infinite possibility. Jimmy defines this foresight as apocalyptic thought and exclaims the intellectual worth of the curiosity involved in this type of thought. Martin, taking in the entire comprehensiveness of the story of humanity, narrates an image of humanity progressing as a whole. He depicts the progression through history as ignorantly capricious, with no distinct idea of what might be a worthy end for Us.//

David: I've been thinking about the beginning and the end. What makes something the beginning and what makes something the end? Besides time? Being beside time? Moving with the feeling of something? Thinking about what's next to do? What is my mission now? At what time do I have to be there? Oops, there's silence now – a strange occurrence in company. Look around the room. They feel that silence too. What's next to do? All this nextality and confusion of what's next to do? That's the question nowadays, so where did it come from? How did we become stuck between the beginning and the end? I can't see that far down the road, but I try. I try to see what my goal is. Yeah, that's what it is: a goal, a story – food for my dreams. I guess that makes sense . . . you need a story to have a moral of the story. And that's about all I hear about around here. He's immoral; she's immoral. The only problem is that most adults don't ask for a story to go along with it. I'm not sure why. So then, how does there exist a goal? How is a story made? How does it develop from beginning to end? What makes it have a goal? Hmm . . . I know have a goal when I lose something because I can't remember where it last was. What was lost at the beginning? What did we WE WE WE WE WE have before? . . . What a surprise: I can't remember.

Martin: BANG! That was a *Big* bang. Suddenly one is not One anymore. Two eyes see one:

Peter: Yes, two eyes see one . . . a strikingly emblematic human quality.

David: I am human. I am the sum of my experiences. I am always experiencing new things. I am always changing. So who am I? Such a strange feeling. Three Dimensions?? Where Am I? Oh, right! The BANG. Fuck – I'm stuck between the beginning and the end. I understand that our existence is something that is necessary to happen. I understand that we are reaching a goal – something new and true. But what I don't understand is all this mean time. What is all this mean time for? What's the hold up?

[*Thoughts*]

Jimmy:
Once came; my name was plain,
With no need or cause to blame.

Twice came; the dwell of shame:
Quirks of the game crumble in tame.

The Cause that contains breaths only through change, and
After great disdain, uncrumbles –
Returns from whence it came.

[*Thoughts*]

Prescott: I understand the feeling of being "stuck," like being teased with glimpses: We encounter only periodic glimpses of the Love we are creating: The Love that holds One the Father and Child. Such a true Love only to be experienced like the tide here on earth. *You never know until it's over, and it's never over until you know. . .*

//David rushes to contemplate the entire breadth of "mean time" between the beginning and the end. He jumps back and forth, relating multiple concepts that had arose in the discussion to the holism of it all. He talks much of what a story involves and finally wonders what could possibly make a story have an end or goal. Mirroring the loss of Oneness after the Big Bang, he claims that when one loses something, there is a compelling reason to find what one has lost. And it is through this experience of "finding" that one truly understands what they have lost. This is an interesting point of the discussion: one cannot appreciate Home, Truth,

Original (whatever you want to call it), until one strays from it and then "return from whence you came." Prescott puts an interesting twist on things with another lesson of Truth: "You never know until it's over, and it's never over until you know." This implicates the uncertainty of "mean time" and caps off perfectly David and Jimmy's wonders with a mind-bending vision when the end of the world and Truth coincide. Also, Martin makes a brilliant observation of how the physically observable qualities of human experience can represent our deepest struggles: the example of two eyes seeing one is fascinating to Peter.//

Martin: I've always enjoy metaphors, such as "the tide," as Prescott put it. They express Truth in similarity and likeness – how things are like or similar to other things in some divine kinship. Somehow these things comfort me, so I seek them:

I see my likeness to the exploding universe on all planes of existence. It is a constant fluctuation between taking in (*experiencing*) and projecting out (*expressing*) the limits of my perception. Inhale: Exhale. Water: Piss. Image: 1000 words. Metaphorically speaking, I have taken many deep breaths, and I could have swore the exhale would last an eternity. But here I go again, taking in another breath – going for another ride. Often the moments I experience don't even let me exhale. I am left to suffocate in my own gasp.

Prescott: Our Light is shown through expression. The inner darkness of refusal is made real through the pain we have now. The inner faith is made real through the Love we have now. Only it is never exactly how it feels now. After all, the moment stops. In the end, Our Light is made through the expression of Our divine experience *in its totality*. You may refuse now if you are standing up instead of lying down, but it will be seen *that nothing in its expressed totality is that of darkness.*

Peter: Expressive truths find themselves in multiple "personalities." In other words, expressions that reflect Truth of being are revealed in a variety of fashions – multiple faces amazingly appreciated by single persons. The most showing, passionate, and uninhibited of these "personalities" are found in music. We adapt to and are consumed by these mindsets, finding comfort in shared experience.

I imagine these progressions as wave patterns that peak and plummet at certain moments of high and low emotional arousal. The uniqueness of each peak or valley is defined by the particular emotion involved and the mental road by which the emotion surfaces. This "mental road" can be physically represented as the actual wave pattern corresponding to the experience. Although criteria for the construction of these waves may be hard to abstract, there are some fundamental associations that may ultimately define the representation:

Peaks and valleys may be achieved gradually or suddenly. The associated emotion may be (from extreme to extreme) tangentially prolonged (plateaus) or erratically unpredictable, which is relatable to the human experience at large, as it expresses itself in multiple "personalities." Also, certain classes of emotions may share a general characteristic of being either a peak or valley.

//Martin brings attention to a key concept: similitude. Not only does he use this concept to generate "truths" about human existence, but he also demonstrates a continuous, natural fluctuation that embodies human experience. This embodiment is crucial because its general vision of experience can be seen in similar fashions pervasively throughout life. He words this fluctuation as "experiencing" vs. "expressing," or, in other words, "taking in" vs. "projecting out," and gives several examples that represent this fluc-tuation. Prescott adds that Truth or "Light" is found in expression.

He refers to "the end," preaching that even the darkest moments of our lives will find Light through the divine expression that results from the unification of all humanity. The statement "Nothing in its expressed totality is that of darkness" is a lesson of ultimate importance preached by Prescott. In terms of humanity's story, this has fundamental implications: certain "scenes," if you will, may be emotionally clouding, so far as to provoke an "inner refusal" of the comprehensiveness of the story as an eventual Whole. When the story is over, however, it will be seen that the story could not have been without these scenes. Peter goes on to recognize music as the truest and most uninhibited form of human expression. He adds a fascinating point that musical expression is appreciated in multiple "personalities." His definition of "personality" is crucial to understanding his proposition. Simply put, he defines personalities as "reaction progressions" to the unlimited variety of experiences provided by life's emotional complexity. Finding comfort in music is another example of how shared (communal) experiences provide inner certainty.//

David: Look to music! The Spirit holder!

//David gets a shot of confidence, as he repeats enthusiastically what he had said previously in the discussion.//

Martin: Yeah Dave, I guess you were ahead of things. I do believe you have incredible foresight, but I'm still trying to see the whole picture. [*Pause*] I think the key concept is similitude. When I can reflect on things that are similar to myself or my experiences, I gain self-knowledge and certainty. Even basic habitual acts can represent definitive qualities of my self. This reminds me of one instance in particular . . . I remember it because it's not often one is fortunate enough to more deeply understand the qualities of his/her self:

Every once in a while there will be a dollar bill of some sort in my pocket, and one might understand the discipline involved in keeping hands out of full pockets. All I need is a little distraction—a conversation of some sort (attention leaves from self to external)—and when my attention returns to what my limbs had been up to while I was gone, I notice the dollar bill has been rolled up (by some part of me) into something looking like a hollow tube. It never fails. But I wonder how hard it really is for some people to keep their hands out of their pockets. Don't we like to ignore? Usually the pants, shirts, and shoes are what matter for the show…these things say who we are, not what's in our pockets. As you might have guessed, I'm a little tired of this show, so if you can't find me, I'll be backstage checking my pockets. Because, you see, my tendencies exists as representations of my *true* self. Not exactly, but similar enough play with.

//Martin reiterates the fundamental concept serving as a gateway to Truth: similitude. He uses another one of his patented "scenarios" to give an example of how very basic acts can represent (in their similitude) qualities of one's true identity. He finishes by saying that the most telling qualities of one's "soul" can be represented by unconscious tendencies, i.e., actions that have become comfortably seated in one's routine(s). The difficult part is separating oneself—being metaconscious in a sense—in order to become aware of these tendencies and reflect on them. In Martin's words, this takes a certain curiosity about knowledge of one's "true" self. "Curiosity" in the discussion has been said to be a definitive quality of a child, so it is relevant to understand the Child, Jesus Christ, as the one perfected curiosity and complete "Meta-Conscious."//

Peter: What is interesting is the pervasive natural tendency of deconstruction and the sometimes following reconstruction. They combine to be a basic existential truth. So then it would not be overly capricious to classify them as opposing sides, or, in other words, claim them to be teleological positives and negatives that essentially reflect positive and negative ends. Although, this supposes some divine purpose that naturally carries with it positive and negative designations in relation to that purpose. Which side is which? There seems to be no fine line.

Prescott: "Which side is which?" Hmm . . . these are the **verges of understanding**. On the verge of understanding you will be overwhelmed by this question: Am I looking at God or the Devil, so to speak? How is the child supposed to reconstruct the fallen pieces without knowledge of the original construct? Maybe the point is simply the attempt to reconstruct.

[*Prescott strikes a chord with everyone*]

Jimmy:
When you spit a line of reason
Beware of those who say treason
Turn around, recollect your spit
Make sure you get each last drip
Get to know what you keep swallowin

//Peter observes a tendency that exists in all humans to some degree of recurrence: Deconstruction and subsequent reconstruction involve the attempt to understand what certain functioning parts comprise the whole (deconstruction) and how those parts might be reconstructed into a comprehensively understandable whole (reconstruction). Peter also plays with the idea of categorizing these tendencies as opposing positives and negatives, i.e., as if these tendencies reflect positive and negative ends if carried to the extreme of divine purpose. Prescott reframes this notion of distinguishing between opposing sides by claiming that they are "verges of understanding." He then remarks on the uncertainty intrinsic to reconstruction, noting that there is no perfect exaction of the original construct – it will only exist in similitude. By placing an emphasis of virtue on the attempt to reconstruct, he implies that reconstruction reflects the positive end – the end of "the child," or the end of Jesus. It follows that reconstruction cannot occur before deconstruction takes place; therefore, Jesus would experience both sides. Prescott would say, however, that Jesus' ultimate emotional motivation is toward reconstruction, with deconstruction simply being a necessary station of passage to the ultimate goal. The negative end (deconstruction) can be more clearly understood as a full concentration, academically speaking, in deconstruction: If one only deconstructs, they will not experience reconstruction and therefore not truly appreciate the integrative and holistic nature of the matter at hand.//

Peter: Now if I may attempt to reconstruct the basic elements of our discussion. It seems we are on the "verge of Truth," so I think it's time to go back – you can only dance around something, talking in circles, for so long before one should notice the point of revolution…

//Peter's notion of a "point of revolution" essentially claims a single, ultimate motive by which everything perpetuates toward completion. It is another development of the concept of the "Spirit."//

Beginning with the symbolic foundation of the "Big Bang," it is absolutely clear that we all conceive of the universe as a pending holistic process (at least from our limited perspective in the meantime). This process is never confused and always perfect in its continuation towards completion. It is agreed that at its culmination of events there will be an arrival at a single, ultimate state of truthful reflection. This truth is the motivation sparking the "Big Bang":

The explosion from a singularity into multiplicity is essential because Truth can only be achieved in community (singularity never "truly" existed). In other words, without any mode of comparison involving *two*-way reflection between self-reflective beings, there can be no substance to identity/Truth:

It is a crucial point that the lonely, encapsulated state of human being is that of uncertainty. Like many feelings, uncertainty can either be the guiding light or the disguising shadow, depending on the interpretation per person. Many suppress uncertainty and seek the superficial certainty of non-eternal, earthly delights. Others curiously follow uncertainty in hope of an infinite, eternal certainty that is Truth.

Upon experiencing, or "taking in," there is a filter, or perceptual buffer, through which we re-present reality in elements of human understanding. This representational process involves a translation from the divine expression of an objective universe to the subjective experience of human being. Martin would call this "taking in" or "experiencing"; however the movement from experiencing to "projecting out" (or expressing) flows on a continuous line, so the two "sides" are essentially indistinguishable:

As initial experiencing soaks in, so to speak, toward higher levels of creative self-reflection, the emotional dynamic of the initial experiential surface may motivate further artistic translations to something that represents in semblance (similitude) the initial superficial (surface) experience. The more uninhibited the formulated translations become, the further down the continuous line one is toward the category of "expression."

As we reflect upon superficial experience, human language provides fundamental structural and relational form to these translations (as fleeting pictorial-like concepts that are all spatially related) and allows for further translation of these concepts into more categorically organized verbal thought. The subjective organization/ translation into verbal thought is where the danger of self-deceit lies. This particular danger of self-deceit is the cause of our discussion's occasional contempt for language. Although language is our basic instrument of expression, we all displayed frustration with it because it is easy to become victims of roads to false translation:

It is often that humans take certainty in misconstrued translations for the purpose of their own earthly operations and objectives, while ignoring the transcendent Truth of an experience guided by ultimate purpose:

Here lie the obstacles to the understanding and sharing of our selves. While similarities are truths, differences remain as threats to many of the close-minded. The natural cultivation of this judging and categorizing-type mentality is our greatest obstacle to the sharing of our selves. Furthermore, we are left with even more preliminary obstacles to the understanding of our true selves:

For one, it takes a certain curiosity to "separate from oneself" so as to understand the tendencies that may represent one's true self (Meta-Conscious). It is prevalent in society that we abandon the understanding of our true selves for the appeal of the persona. Not only is it common to keep some aspects of our true selves in secret, but it is also impossible to portray all aspects with justice and proportionate resistance to external expectations. The problem becomes that individuals might come to identify more with their persona than their true self, essentially living a false life.

We have tried adamantly to be slow and careful in our translations – trying to inch closer to the "perceptual buffer" that, in a sense, clouds objective reality. This explains our discussion's tendency of using images as an initial conceptual basis before any expanded verbal translation began.

The fact that our experience requires constant representation (meaning presenting again after translation) is crucial: Representations can only provide *similitude* to the original presentation. As we have discussed, *similitude* is the building block of Truth:

Finding similarities between and through all representations allows us to become certain of a singular nature through which everything originates. This nature is inexpressible in word (obviously) but might be generally described as the essence of motivational identity that the discussers (Us) might name (for the sake of play) the unchanging Spirit behind the continuous perpetuation of our divine process of expression. It follows that our Trinitarian objectives give shape to the general embodiment of our quest toward Truth:

*The "Father" is the point of Origin from which Truth is expressed and from which the "Child" is exploded. Everything separated by time and space from the Original is in some way a reflection of that Original. Humanity is the embodiment of this eternal reflection of the Original's Truth, as we are the language bearers who are destined to unify into a state of perfect Truth by reflecting through and between each others' similarities.

*The "Child" is that which lives in divine reflection of the point of Origin. The "Child" grows away from the Original but has innate (but perhaps not always conscious) awareness of the singular nature of all progressions (Original providing): The "Child"'s identity equals that of the "Father," for the nature of the Original singularity is inseparable from its spawn. But any certain Truth of identity must be reflected among multiple, that is, with available comparison; therefore the necessity of birth and the evolution of beings who can communicate through language, eventually leading to a perfected, unified, and communal state of Truth: Humanity, in complete unification, is the Body of Life, which has obviously yet to be fully collected and assembled. As for Christ incarnate, we suppose his role is the medium through which all souls are truthfully presented in unison: He is without judgment, extracting the essence of each individual's link as it contributes to Truth. Metaphorically speaking, Jesus' unique sunglasses allow him to look directly at the Sun (source of light/Truth).

*Upon recollection (collecting backward, increasing togetherness, toward One), the guiding <u>Holy Spirit</u> binds eternal the "Father & Son" – reflecting on and through each other in infinite Truth. That would about wrap it up, wrapping us up, sort of like DNA.

Martin: I look a lot like you Dad.

Prescott: And so we are truly made in the image of God: When I am consumed with Love—full of positive end—I, like the Universe, am reaching *in all* directions.

[*A collective mental wOw*]

Jimmy: I don't know, it's like . . . .well, . . . uhhhh, . . . I guess that's about all I can say: I don't *know*, it's *like* _____

[*Collective, unrestrained laughter*]

//[Laughter]//

Afterward

What is a thought without an afterthought? One might digest the discussion as a series of afterthoughts; however, the reader would not want to look back on the discussion without giving full credit to the authenticity involved in the fluid revelation (and recollection/ reconstruction-following) that makes up the story of *one* thoughtful event. Yes, the discussion did include multiple thoughts, but what is more important is its revolving around *one* spirited pursuit – possibly said as the desire to collect and unite.

But to unite what with what, or who with whom? At this particular after-point, that answer should be flowing. Now is simply a time to exhale; the tributaries of such a flow will hopefully reveal themselves in time and marked sections.

For all practical purposes, this afterward marks a distinct moment of changing gears to digest the emotional flows, strategies, and self-evaluations that allow unrestrained experiences of creativity to recur in daily life without repercussions of undisciplined thought patterns, social withdrawal, or the general feeling of being weird and out of touch. Not only does this afterward present tactics for designing a so called releasable/retractable leash for keeping track of thoughts that stretch the limits of imagination, but intellectual reflections are explored with attention to those introspectively creative moments when the leash guiding such an uncertain imaginary venture becomes retracted. These intellectual afterthoughts serve to translate the personally unique into something "they" have to confront and recognize as having communal/social relevance. To be sure, "they" will dismiss unruly thoughts on grounds of non-accommodation to comprehensible social terms and lack of will to understand the individual; so in creative discipline, it is imperative to reach out to accommodate others in order to prevent the severing of ties with the majority's terms because the majority does rule – certainly. And if you completely sever ties with the majority, its rules will haunt you; they will haunt you to an unlivable end. In this sense, to avoid the unlivable end, one can outline the project of *designing one's sanity*, and hopefully the examples herein might be a teacher to others that get lost in dark regions and are trying to find their way back home.

The reader should also be aware that this entire work was very gradually organized after being a scattered expressive outlet during a time of adolescent internalization. That being said, the afterward is not so often explanatory of how the story behind the course of one's ideas represents the underlying tactics of how one's sanity becomes designed, refined, and maintained; rather, the afterward will often be openly expressive, that is, non-intentional. Although explanations are given—here and there—it's important to maintain a moderated dosage of such tediously controlled and constructed explanations in effective teaching. The delicate balance between spoon-fed explanations and more abstract presentations, like scaffolding, allows the teacher to essentially place an idea on the learner's shoulder in order to provoke the student to turn their own head and *find it for themselves* (as opposed to shoving "it" in their face, which has been my common experience in this era of educational institutions).

P.S. If you are fascinated by the hypothetical person that was Jesus, you will enjoy checking out the less abstract and more intellectually applicable analyses of His/his complicated being as the supposed savior of the world, which comprises one of the later sections of the afterward. If you are so curious, it may reveal some "down-to-earth" observational techniques that are useful to examine His/his Person/person from a base and logical perspective.

The General Rule of Impatience

General Rule:

I desire the growth of my person. As I *reach in all directions*, my ultimate desire is to absorb and take in *everything* and *everyone*. As follows through everyday, my creative eye toward all dimensions absorbs/takes in [the situation I find myself in] as a *whole* – one scene, one experience, one truth. My goal becomes to recognize this functioning whole as embodied in a clear metaphorical scheme, whereby my familiarity with such a scheme can facilitate the analysis of each significant part of that whole scene. Once I have both seen the situation as a whole and analyzed it parts, I can venture to discover a general rule as it applies to my situation of repetitious being. I may discover the unforeseen recurrences that tell me about who I am, where I am, and why I am here – as a general rule.

I take in the *whole* situation, analyze its parts, start my general rule, but am then stopped by the devil's advocate. Now that I have stopped, I take in a new *whole*, seeing my previous whole-taking self taking in the previous whole so that I might make a new, further developed general rule. But I am not satisfied – no conclusion is reached: I stop again to see a new whole, that of myself looking on the self that is looking on the self that was taking in the original whole, and so on.[11] So I kill myself to find the general rule of all general rules, perpetually in search of the observer on high.

---

[11] See section: **The Overseer, the Overseen, and the Overseeant**

We stop to find the general rule to be satisfied in conclusion, and until this satisfaction in conclusion, we wish not act again. So then we decide to conclude so that we may act again – to survive. We act again and find more general rules . . . So where is my beginning, and what is my general rule? Did my first act of being follow the conclusion of a general rule or vice versa? Can we act without conclusion of a general rule to follow? Is light found in the fluidity of uninterrupted action or the herky-jerky stop-and-go of retrospect toward general rule? And if light is found through the resulting general rule, it must then be dependent on the recurrence of action (co-dependence). The only thing is that no matter how many general rules you find and no matter how far you ascend to the observer on high, you will still fall a sleep, you will still wake up, and you will still take action like the dumb human fuck that you are . . . and the general rule that you found once before and thought had changed you forever, returns to laugh in your face, saying *"who's your daddy?"*

Impatience:

There is no greater impatience/frustration than these processes of realizations: Daily self-observations, *recurring* over several days, several months, or several years, cause you to understand the childish pace of your progress in whatever (understanding, maturing, growing, achieving, developing, etc.). The ultimate direction of your progress becomes clearly deducible, as you *foresee your own end*. The child foresees his end and wishes to speed up his pace to the ultimate of ultimates—to get to the point—only to realize that he possesses no such agency and remains but a feeble child – a follower. It is like if you were ever enrolled in a class where the reading was of a book you had read a thousand times before. But you still have to sit through class . . . to get the grade – to survive for some reason. But I survive to end. I survive to ascend. So in this class, of earth sciences, I stare impatiently at the clock . . . the bell is surely about to ring. . .

CREATIVE DISCIPLINE

There comes a time in one's life when one begins to absorb their being, and its relation to *all* being, with a profoundly extended openness: One's creative imagination dreams of its peak to maximum absorption – to a place of no limits. These dreams may become realized-as-unreal and impracticable, they may be entertained with endless hope, or likely both contradictory attitudes about these dreams may become sustained in frustrated limbo.

I heard somewhere that hope is the best of things. But with extreme hope comes the crashing blow of reality, so then it becomes the objective of creative discipline to manage these two opposing attitudes (hope and realization) into a maximization of *personal* imaginary satisfaction and *social* productivity in the form of *one* livable bond.

To summarize or state an important general rule of this management: *If intellectual analysis does not follow one's most ridiculously and personally true creations, then you have no leash.* And dogs without leashes get run over by commercial trucks, as if there were no place in their world for such disturbances. Secondly, *the feeling of "going crazy," in general, is often just the result of coming to believe that you might be "crazy."* There is nothing wrong with entertaining thoughts; we only become disturbed by ideas of craziness when we see ourselves entertaining "unruly" thoughts and perceive a separation between oneself and others. So the creative one who comes to feel forever alone in his own world should hold off on that lonely belief…be assured that your return is awaited with curious envy...We could use your company here on the ground.

Recognition of Being:

There are certain moments—maybe even everyday—that bring one to recognize the ridiculousness of one's existence...a dumbfounded recognition of being. The simple fact that *you* are *one* point of view, living *through* the confinements of a physical body is absolutely surreal. Such bare recognition of one's being is not easy to come by, as the opportunity for such recognition seems to be naturally detoured by the lure to sustain narrowly focused attention – the siren of society: So we involve ourselves in dedication to remarkably singular objectives which require moving in straight mental lines. From one point to the next, we move toward foreseen objectives in the straightest of possible lines so to be sure of not becoming lost...

To recognize your being, you must first lose yourself. Mental lines are no longer straight, but zigzags of all directions venturing to a place never before seen. This far-off venture allows for the possibility of a self-discovering rendezvous with one's original home of being that one had left, lost, and now returned to find:

As the story goes—alone—one has become lost in imaginary presences – to a world without words. Its fantastic story may culminate or be interrupted—either/or—which essentially comes to define the smoothness of one's eventual return to superficial engagements. The return landing might be symphonically conclusive, harshly abrupt, or somewhere in between. If one happens to be lucky enough to conclude, word presentations will likely erupt to give the experience a character of general rule or verbal satisfaction in conclusion (or verbal unsettling conclusion), but it is certainly not that easy. Concluding a creative experience with the discovery of an ultimate general rule is rare relative to the number of imaginations one engages in, so with creative discipline one learns to appreciate the vast majority of our creations that stop short, as they become disorganized or interrupted:

When interruption occurs, it is marked by a shortage of word presentations, that is, there is a lack of words needed to recap the experience. There is a speechless frustration, as the end (or general rule) is left on the tip of one's tongue.[12]

At the same time, it is possible to lack the achievement of a general rule and still be far-gone from the "real" surface of being. So then, when your person is far removed in some imaginary world and becomes suddenly interrupted, you have the chance enjoy the experience of *recognition of being*, that is if you leave space in time to stop, look out the window of the traversing stunt plane, and recognize the qualitative difference between imaginary and real worlds. This transfer of worlds is sure to happen – just stop[13] and recognize.

Routine – First & Second Nature:

When something has become routine, it can be done without thinking; it has become *second nature*. Conveniently my second nature can take its course while I, my first nature, takes my own – my mind is elsewhere. It might be said that routine is boring, and this is certainly so, but there are also certainly times when things have to be done . . . work before play. So in these mean times between work and play my mind becomes elsewhere whenever the routine of work permits. I gain the opportunity to contemplate my first nature as my second nature does the rest: I have forgotten myself, I have no body, and I live in a world all to my own.

The routine of work and bodily movement is nothing new. So the creative one, who constantly seeks new things and new truths,

---

[12] That is until you have mastered "verbal sparsing," (See sub-section: *Vocabulary*) in which case you might have the skill to *pick up where you left off.*

[13] See sub-section: *Meta-Conscious*

departs his attention away from such things of second nature to the parallel world of new and true things – his first nature.

The routine of chit-chat and greeting new faces is also nothing new, yet these never before seen faces that are the subjects of routine communication are sadly the newest of all news – not to be taken routinely. So the creative one, in ecstatic anticipation of new soulful contact, has the pure ambition to banish all routines from verbal accessibility in respect of and wonder for each new person he meets. Sadly, this anticipation is too impatient and too ambitious because the majority of new faces humbly expects and desires first meetings to be routine so to be sure of initial agreement, as superficial as that agreement might be.

The creative one leaves superficial bulls&%t to the mute world of routine. With desire for everything but her creative will to takes its course without conscious effort (as if everything but her will to create was a waste of time), the creative one's creativity begins to speak and live, and her routines of daily life become mute and dead. As the creative one gains the will to act more, the world of routine becomes further removed in distance from the creative world. The two worlds essentially become *qualitative* opposites. In other words, the creative one *feels* one world to be life and the other to be death: Creation is conscious, with feeling, and willful; routine, on the other hand, is unconscious, without feeling, and without will.

In setting aside one's creative will in order to access the world of routine, the creative one must go through a mental reorganization process. If she is so consumed by her own world, this reorganization can be such a drastic change in mental structure and intention that the creative one, upon attempting to reorganize, may become dumbfounded and feel seemingly cut off from the narrow world of routine. And so one might reflect on the stagnant feeling of being speechless, motionless, or caught between two directions – wondering of where one was supposed to be headed.

Action:

What is commonly understood as "action" in the physically productive sense of speech, movement, or the general influence over external things, as well as its antecedent "to ponder," for lack of a better word, will be understood oppositely in the context of this afterward. Common logic will tell you that "pondering" concludes before one decides to move or *act*; however, in this context it will be the curious mental state of "pondering" that represents *action*. In these curious states of mental activity the person is no longer a follower, as she pauses to become her own creator.

Creative absorption gives the intake action. In many ways, creative openness is the development and elaboration of the story behind any word/idea – there is action behind the scenes, and so the play becomes more meaningful. One might reflect on the stagnant and unfulfilling conversations in which the other person's words simply lack much behind the scenes – their understanding is *passive* recollection, their creative will is non-existent, and they are stubbornly seated in some scheme of understanding that derives itself from a history of passive subordination to a convenient group of subject-matter "authorities." They have rejected growth, so there is no leeway to communicate, and souls fail to make contact.

The desire to quickly give something a word feels like an "active" accomplishment and can be quite satisfying, but this kind of "quick wit" is often just a fearful desire to avoid action – to avoid pure thought in creative elaboration.

Objects & Objectives:

The progress of creative action begins to halt as soon as the experience being absorbed is given a name. Assigning a name or label is always derived from ulterior motives/objectives that are nearly impossible to keep logically consistent across personal assertions or beliefs. The aim of creative action, on the other hand, is to discover and capture the true essence of human expression so as to learn a consistent truth behind the origin of *all* creation. Like the universe, the creative one reaches in all directions: she dreams without boundaries – without names. If Truth ever reaches a name, it is not assigned until *all* is sure, seen, collected, and recollected. Prematurely given names are assigned by the imperfection of humanity – in search of power, permanence, and control.

We take what we hear (those words) and we take what we see (those faces) as objects. Their aura of permanence fortifies our thought representations so that they are livable, stationary, and able to be *counted on*.[14] We guard against change, uncertainty, and difference; we meet these threats of change with intolerance and thwarts to exile. With objective boundaries we encapsulate and see things within the within of all withins as if it were its own personal within. Without caring to wonder about the "within of all withins," we take what we hear and what we see as single objects that are permanent to themselves; thus promoting the egocentric desire to exclude and the unwillingness to see all singles as part of an interconnected whole. All of our single things, concepts, and even soulful faces are cast away from the true Whole and horribly (even worse certainly) judged within contextual objectives – ulterior motives.

The ulterior lure of contextual objectives is perhaps clearest during discussions of how the "mind" works, if you have them. Too often a person will fall back to the haven of objectification in an anal attempt to cage the most abstract and un-cageable of concepts: They rush to give **it** a name – "brain."

The label "brain" is clearly much more permanent than "mind" because "brain" associates to a very clear, singular object that has definitive boundaries (the "organ" itself); furthermore, **it** is referred

---

[14] Taking something as an object is the pursuit of giving it a coat of simplified presentation. Bordered and simplified, the coat stabilizes the concept to more swiftly and narrowly function through contextual objectives. Coats only function through earthly objectives . . . What wears the coat, and the dresser of the wearer, are left to another world – the world of creation.

to as "brain" by renowned intellectuals who achieve their desired objectives of producing cures, successful experiments, etc. We see these achievements and gain a certain comfort in the certainty of perceived absolute knowledge about the concept in question and its so called name.

The concept of "mind," on the other hand, tends to associate to a curiously heightened state of introspection – to the bare awareness that is the self-conscious soul. Then it frequently becomes tempting in abstract discussions (such as "how the mind works") to see the concept in question through the lens of an external reference frame *who* objectifies the concept and gives it clear boundaries, thereby ending all fears of disintegration, uncertainty, and loss of *control*. And so we *cling* to know the world through its objects therein because, as we all know, objects are under control. Having permanent boundaries, our objects remain forever to be *counted on*, as we live to be certain that they will never die . . .

The ungodly fear of death . . . as we run away from active subjectivity, our discussions become passive, ulterior, avoiding the internal self, and submitting to the objectives of various external authorities that have provided us with such lovely objects to idolize.[15] And if a creative, more active soul attempts to draw the passive one into a less border-controlled realm of self-examination, he will run and run for certain – back to his trusty objects.

Pride:

Creative elation is an all-consuming experience. With such inspiring emotion, *the creative one needs no words to move along with the story of her creation*, allowing one the freedom to venture

---

[15] When push comes to shove, the objects you take will die. You will cry upon seeing for the first time that they are not the immortal objects you took them to be. So one would be advised to take only One object because only One thing remains when all is collected and assembled. The Body will not breathe in full until only One object is taken . . . false idols are everywhere.

far into the space of the unknown. One's truth is beautiful, but *the more abstractly one moves, the harder it will become to give that story word because the possibilities of translation approach* ∞. It can be an excruciating process to destroy such purity and filter into word, so *the ultimate temptation of the creative one is to cut the line that makes her leash.* Some may try to cut the line with all of their heart but to no avail. And when they fall back to the leash-holder[16] (reality, society, obligation, etc.), they will have forgotten who they are, beginning an excruciatingly complicated case of recognition of one's being . . . the bruises one suffers from such a fall may take some time to heal, so patience is certainly a virtue.

The length of one's leash does in fact have a limit, but its purpose is not to reinforce the correctness of fearful subordination to some higher power; rather, it serves you – to prevent you from death, that is, pride. Pride seeks one's personal gain or reverence and ignores the equality of persons in whose relationship states the being of *all* creation. The man of pride has left us all, for himself.[17]

Guilt:

In the early times of one's growth, when the emotions that accompany creativity are new experiences, the creative one, upon reaching her emotional destination, may fall in love – head over heals. Having never known Love before, there seems to be nothing that can control such boiling impetuousness. The young adult begins to estimate her autonomous potential to ascend/discover and falls in Love with this potential of oneself – the self on the way to ascension.

---

[16] At this point it is possible that "kite-holder" is the more appropriate metaphor because the 'falling' aspect is an important component, as gravity will strike hard if you cut the line. On the other hand, for general purposes the leash image strikes a chord because it implies certain intentions of the leash-holder.

[17] See sub-section: *Pride Vs. Humility*

But life is not one long ascension period . . . the human falls. We are most often stuck to the mean time or latency periods.

Latency periods are the times when guilt comes down on the creative one because she is separated from her Love: Her current state of being stands in contrast to the end-state of creative ascension that she tries and cries to remember.[18] The memory will not come, as her attention is divided—her Love is divided—and so guilt comes down. This particular type of guilt is surely unpleasant; it may, nevertheless, still be seen as a necessary chapter in the story of the long-term growth of the creative one.

Look at it this way: The present "you" is one person, the creative throne is another person, and latency guilt is another person. The latency guilt person is there to stay on your tail – he oversees your emotional state (or lack there of) in order to keep the commitment to creativity strong and ensure the next rendezvous with one's Love who waits on the creative plateau. Latency guilt and the next return to manifest creation can be a perilous cycle—one difficult to manage—so another aim of the creative one is to become acquainted with the guilt person, moreso upon each time he returns. Because in furthering your acquaintanceship, the natural reaction to dwell in your hate for the guilt person will diminish.

Toward the end of proper acquaintanceship, *the guilt person should ideally be a reminder, that is, something positive within your present state that reminds you of who you are and where you have been.* He should **not** bring self-deprecation. Although his appearance might be that of an opposer, his essential purpose is so closely tied to the identity of the creative one, that the two ultimately cannot be separated.

---

[18] This onset of guilt is distinctly different from that of the average, passive person. This type of guilt is from the circumstantial *lack* of creativity, whereas the passive person feels guilty in the *presence* of creative activity because he ventures to break the rules, that is, the things he has felt necessary to accept his whole life.

Intellectualization:

Creativity allows one to experience <u>new</u> *emotional states of understanding.* Consequently, one's path of engagement will present the daunting task of structuring the post-recollection of that state into word, for nothing new yet has a word, and so you grow, and so the word grows, and Truth is word.

Reiterating, there is a natural human inclination toward passivity, that is, to limit our experience to those states we have simple words for because this keeps us close to home – places we know and have known for certain. Conversely, the creative one, upon opening the door of her home, sees the beauty that waits afar in the distance. There are no marked paths, so the venture is bold; nonetheless, the undying hope remains, as the creative one begins the growth of her word and the story behind it. So this brings us to the dangerous faculty of a word when it grows beyond emotional control:

Intellectual analysis is the blunting of emotion. This frame of mind essentially takes an idea and strips it of its emotional character in order to restrain oneself and maintain some kind of even keel. Its use is so common and naturally adaptive that its function is often executed outside of awareness, or at least without being aware of its purpose to steer oneself away from emotion. For example, a doctor might explain that someone has "expired" instead of "died" in order to maintain a mindframe of professional performance that might otherwise be compromised in the face of emotion. While certain professional pursuits might be forms of intellectual truth, creative elation involves the establishing of an emotional truth (whether combined with intellect or not). So it follows that intellectual analysis is the objective opposite of the emotional center of creativity. Nevertheless, anti-emotional intellectual analyses remain a complementary necessity of mental survival.

As the creative one grows, interconnections of emotional truths make her prone to spontaneously relive (as if the trigger becomes itchier) the essence of past creative moments. These moments are triggered as an opportunity for the creative one to inspect the profundity and entire life that breaths through these past (and now binding with the present) creative moments of emotional truth. Being emotionally overwhelmed and speechless as a result of these revelations becomes a tricky and elusive state to handle. It can leave at any moment – impurely interrupted: it may leave one stunned and unable to find one's surface routines. So when these moments arise, one must sustain the carefully curious eye—slow to translate or conclude—for only through one's gentle slowness will She remain – Her beauty makes her ever shy.[19]

So we must attempt to learn the art of slow inspection: It becomes like a relationship that at first might be uneasy, confusing, or overwhelming, but as time goes by the anxiety subsides and a peaceful relationship of mutual understanding is established.

As sad as it may be, still, the art requires management, and the creative virgin, so to speak, might not recognize the appropriate time to turn around. It is true that it can be beneficial to one's mental strength to decide *against* turning around, that is, it might be the best way to learn what exactly is "too far." But in time, for one's own maturity and health in management, it will be absolutely necessary and utterly dependent on your barest of consciousness to decide when it is proper to turn around: Here, it is most important to know that it will be up to **you** to recognize when you have gone too far, and there is no perfect stopping point. No one can be told when to stop, but there does come a time (for some strange reason) when it is healthy to come back and remember what you have been taught and the others that surround you. But also remember that **you** are the untaught.[20] And true education is unteaching.

---

[19] Amazing is the one who is not speechless upon Her return – instead manic with verbal outflow and fast with conclusion. This one is amazing but surely overzealous. I beg against fast conclusion; it scares Her to death, and at this she leaves fast and runs away . . . this is not the way to part with infinite beauty.

[20] I look to the top for confirmation – to whomever's body in which it now resides. I shout at the podium, "They look to you and not themselves. Do you see this?" I look to the top, saddened with guilt, to find that it is he at the top who I deride. I am forced to depart alone. I am left to teach myself.

Vocabulary:

Acquiring new vocabulary is a primary resource utilized by the intellectualization process. Vocabularies that incorporate a variety of contexts allow the same essence of meaning to be presented through different contextual objectives. Because the creative one has the most pure and ideal objective of including everyone, translating her unadulterated concepts into a variety of seemingly foreign contexts can be an excruciating filter through which to grate one's essences. Nonetheless, dedication to this excruciation can give birth to the important development of *contextual versatility*, through which the creative one can imagine a *variety of companies*. This allows, still, the development of uniquely personal concepts, but at the same time helps prevent crashes of loneliness.

A variety of imaginary companies becomes a resource of reflection that brings the personal uniqueness of creative thought back to a certain social surface where the *expectation of the future input of others* does not die. Conversely, the *withdrawn* creative one has gone so far with her own ideas, *alone* and without looking back for company, that she cries upon seeing the distance she has traveled from anyone that might appreciate her ideas.[21] As was mentioned previously, *the creative one needs no words to move along with the story of her creation*. This is an awesome capacity, but it can also be a dangerous venture through unmarked space. For this reason there are buoys in the ocean, and for the same reason it's possible to adopt a strategy here termed '*verbal sparsing*':

As the creative one moves toward new understandings, she no doubt moves with an array of abstract notions. As these notions grow together, they will fall on a logical line or in logical space. If one's self-awareness is strong enough to recognize such calculated movements toward a new understanding (which takes practice),

---

[21] After all, the most important thing is to share: with good friends who too feel these wordless moments, you will feel Love. And with Love you will move forward.

then one can distinguish between each individual abstract notion as each grows together in space and moves toward a greater conclusion. These points of distinction are where verbal sparsing plays its role:

It is essential in the effort toward designing one's sanity to recognize and give word to one's abstract notions at *intermittent points* in creative ventures. Essentially, each point becomes a memory landmark for subsequent or semi-parallel intellectualization processes; that is, the landmarks lay foundations for the afterward process of trying to pick up the pieces and recollect one's new understanding. *Verbal sparsing allows you to move swiftly through space, avoid premature intellectualizations, and lay foundations for future intellectual re-organizations.*

A true-to-life example of this strategy as shown through an email sent to a Philosophy Professor by a student germinating this particular type of awareness:

Hi Professor,

I wanted to get some input on an idea I had developing today. It wasn't motivated by my paper, but I would still like to know what you think: At first I thought the unconscious to be like the song, and "you" are the dancer. That's pretty vague, but I like to start out that way. . . To encompass individual differences, I was then thinking: everybody has their own style, their own dance, but you still have to play off the same beat. But then I was trying to take into account that parts of the unconscious are collective—of all humans—and other parts are influenced by individual experiences/genetic predispositions or whatever. At first I thought the collective unconscious to be the base, fundamental beats that make up the spirit of the song, with the individual unconscious supplying intermediate beats, possibly through an individual array of instruments. But then I thought what might be most important is that we all inevitably come back to the same chorus or refrain. So I am left to wonder how far individuals are separated in between refrains? As far as my thought process went,

I guess I have the habit of making creative "leaps." But I think it's better to leap far and be wrong than to not leap at all . . . I'm sure you can understand the value in guessing wrong and turning around to pick up the pieces. I also have this strategy that when I think I'm onto something profound but the linguistic details are too crowded and bunched together, I try not to alter that cloudiness, so I attach it to a vague word or title that makes more sense to *me* than anything socially comprehensible. I think the word attachment allows my curiosity to retrieve the idea more easily in the future, while the vagueness of the word leaves the original idea unadulterated for my later return to inspection. So then, when I learn about new shit, I can give that original idea new and more proper light. That's all I have for now. What do you think? No hurry . . . thanks for the time.

Meta-Conscious:

Creativity, and its quality of absorbing a wide scope of things, takes on the property of being "meta-conscious" when such a scope is absorbing the proceedings of one's own person.[22] As one's person proceeds into daily engagements, the motivations and objectives underlying those processes can seemingly arise out of nowhere. As we are carried down paths of nowhere motivations, it can be the will

---

[22] Creative 'ascension' is either a self-over-*self* or self-over-*world* dilation to take in the scope of many things at one moment. Meta-consciousness, in particular, is the self-over-self version of creative ascension. While these states both involve an experience of wide scope, the practice of 'leashing' or designing one's sanity involves essentially the opposite of ascension, as it deconstructs, into pieces, what you were taking in as a whole. In a sense the leash pulls you down from the ascension . . . ascensions **do** end: they can and often do leave you hanging from a limb. These strategies will carry you safely down the tree to the real, the stable, and the livable – a most delightful recognition of being.

of the Meta-Conscious to STOP[23] the moving self and wonder about the thing(s) that owns the motive(s) behind one's path of existence.[24]

Mental proceedings are nothing but capricious. They come and go, in stages yet continuous. They are elusive so as to own your person without a trace and keep your path in a kind of oblivious tangential slavery. Freedom lies only the point where all tangents begin – where oversight is pure. The beauty of the Meta-Conscious is its ability to rise above tangents and distinguish between human stages of thought that otherwise seem to envelop your person like *one* river.

Gaining acquaintance with one's Meta-Conscious develops a *versatile* awareness of different mental states. It provides one with talent to recognize thoughts as they begin to arise and where the originality of such thoughts are likely to take oneself – forging down associative paths that have been ingrained in the past.

We are all ingrained and inspired by the past, and by so we become subject to habitual inspirations behind the arising of our thoughts, and so forth we move to constantly relive these habits of thought. *Now*, as we begin to fall to the associative paths that have become solidified by the emotional inspirations behind ill-gotten habitual thoughts, the fall is best deterred close to the source, as the original thought has begun its scheme. The inspirational origins behind

---

[23] Do not be misled by the bold presentation of '**stopping**': Such an emphasis on STOP might imply a road to mental stagnation; on the contrary, a critical objective is to control and gain strength over the ill effects of such stagnations. At the same time, these stoppages are necessary for personal growth and knowledge of self, ultimately moving toward a further developed meta-conscious acquaintanceship: creative equilibrium. Creative equilibrium—when the Meta-Conscious becomes serenely simultaneous with one's fluid action—one is truthfully living in two simultaneous worlds. Entertaining prolonged stoppages and interrupting this great achievement of equilibrium is worthwhile only when something new cannot be ignored because of its potential for groundbreaking interconnections of truth.

[24] There are times of serious stagnation in the life of the creative one who knows herself: It becomes hard to let herself be because she sees herself being.

the large variety of human thoughts are extraordinarily difficult to distinguish between, so the most daunting task of developing meta-conscious versatility leads to the question: *where are you coming from and where are you going?*

Properly developed *versatility* also involves a keen understanding of how the present mental circumstance requires transition to a particular meta-conscious level of oversight to harness that circumstance, which of course all depends on the nature of the preceding thought. In other words, this is partly a process of coming to master one's leash, allowing a quicker realization of what circumstances require which proper tactic of leash retraction.

Although it is not all bad to release and experience an unsustainably extreme circumstance, the haphazard human may attach to the profundity of this extreme and seek it out endlessly in disregard of other mental survival requirements. Hopefully such haphazard mentalities produce the learning experience of being able to recognize when one is directed down such unlivable paths, which in turn might incite further practice to help one become more keenly aware of what meta-conscious level is appropriate to organize livable ebb and flow.

New differentiations of mental proceedings are monumental developments of self-knowledge and awareness: The effort required to encapsulate a stage of thought and differentiate a stage (as its own) from what appears to be one stream of thought shows bold openness to personal growth as well as wonderfully new capacities to relive.[25]

---

[25] We all love to relive the personal truths that we have known before. Sadly, we are often quick to cement all that is 'known before' as infallible for ease of identity establishment. On the other hand, the creative one, who constantly seeks new differentiations, will find the new and relive the new, moving her curious mind onto more news – she remains alive.

The Noun & the Verb:

One of the most valuable learning experiences can be found in the struggle to translate a language of familiarity into a foreign language. Often we become so fluent in our familiarities that we forget to think . . . before we speak.

In the struggle to translate *what is meant to be said* we are presented with the opportunity to inspect the original essence of what is truly/humanly wished to be expressed and how the hazy, nonverbal origin of such thought has an infinite number of potential verbal translations, of which none are perfect. Unfortunately, this struggle to translate does not always inspire heightened awareness of one's origin of thought, just a frustration with the need to accommodate others. Some may become stubbornly frustrated, impatient, and intolerant of the need to accommodate another language. They ignore the outside and embrace themselves.

When ethno/ego-centrism is set aside, we can recognize and understand the translation from human to culture – from the purity of unlabeled *thought* to the *language* of society. Careful attention to the translation from thought to language is absolutely divine because frustration about such a struggle to translate has no possibility of being ethnocentric: We are all human! One can never be too human-centric. Remaining focused on one's thought instead of the word that might follow is to be at the center of humanity and the untranslated universal grammar that marks the base of how thoughts arise before the mind's eye.

As we push related ideas into structured sentences there are points of translation when we are forced to decide on the order in which these ideas will be presented. This so called "order shuffling" is a process that will often take its course based on the ideas' subject of expression, its objective toward conclusion, or should I say the sentence models that are recalled to seem appropriate. In this sense, we are affected by the present situation and whatever past references we might assimilate to be proper to that situation. To certain degrees, the act of recovering appropriate sentence models is an external reliance on imitation, as opposed to the originality of internal inspection. Although external reliance and imitation are quite necessary and unavoidable when adapting and making social contributions, such *habits* can destroy the creative will and more importantly the meta-conscious desire to know oneself.

In the midst of "shuffling" is when we have the opportunity to stop and recognize the essence of our ideas and how externally imposed objectives have a way of manipulating their original order. It is certainly a difficult task to harness the order and stages that comprise such shuffling because, like most of life's engagements, we can move far distances without recognizing the path we took. So it is necessary to call attention to the parts of speech, utilizing them as the basis for strategic development of meta-conscious oversight in regard to idea-to-word translations:

Specifically the translation from verb to noun-form can shed new light on depth of meaning. Let us take for example the word "anticipating." If I were to narrate a scene and say "This man is anticipating her return," the scene itself is not still, as the presence of verb-form creates for the listener an anticipation of what will happen next (her return), as the man in the scene who is anticipating is only a single part of an extended scene that is sure to *change*: the scene is *moving*. On the other hand, if I were to say "This man is consumed with anticipation," the attention shifts to the essence of the *unchangeable* quality or state that defines anticipation. I could also say, "This man is anticipatory;"[26] however, the new verbal objective that is intrinsic to the adjective part of speech is to define the man, which tends to be an ill-gotten pursuit.

---

[26] This is a perfect example of language difference. Spanish would accommodate this situation with the versatility of 'ser' & 'estar,' that is, by being able to show that this man is *temporarily* in a state of anticipation (anticipatory). In English, however, one might imply a characteristic to be eternal by using 'is,' even if not so intended.

There is substantial depth to be learned from verb-to-noun translations: By taking on the quality of unchangeableness that is intrinsic to noun-form, we gain the meta-conscious focus needed to inspect the essence of an idea – in quest of the original. Ironically, we may again see that a traditional representative of what is thought to be "action" (the verb) does not necessarily tell the whole story. Without soaking in the translation process, one might become duped by the *appearance* of action and never truly act to see the story behind the word.

Balance in Three Persons:

Within a certain conceptual framework and mode of awareness, one can come to recognize a creative balance that resonates under one's surface of being. The manifestation of this balance struggles through traditional cognitive resistance – stubbornly latent until something new and/or lovely familiar lights it on fire to finally glow for one's conscious delight and meta-conscious observational ecstasy. It is a beautiful fire, from its ignition to the final dwindle, and in its beauty—its yearn to be bright—a *three person balance* can be seen: Never a thought of the other as other, it is interplay of pure equality and divine conservation. Never was one without the other, and never was the third without the two. With cupped hands that held to share, *fusion was left for two*:

The uprising of a creative experience involves the attention to *one whole*. This prolonged attention to one whole experience requires a *Creative Experience Holder* who unites the original experience of the recent past with the conscious wonder of the ever-moving present. In this sense, She *holds together the past, present and future* within one collective stream of attention. And certainly when She holds, She holds for another: With cupped hands She holds up her gift to Her partner in Truth for referential reflection. Her partner, in turn, assimilates the creative stream into His array of reference frames. He is the *Objective Observer* (or keeper of external reference frames) who *accepts the gift presented* and the two become unified in perfect reflection: The new creative experience is assimilated into the reference frame that captures its truth – the truth of similitude.

Where there are two in unison, there is a third that unites. The Objective Observer has an endless array of reference frames so to account for the uncountable number of situational directions and requirements that the Creative Experience Holder finds herself in and becomes forced to grasp. The third person—the *Logician—finds the path* to the one appropriate frame (or multiple interrelated frames – sometimes in a comparative trial-and-error process), streamed in the logic of similitude and unifying the two in the beauty of mutual understanding – *fusion was left for two.*

From the intellectual perspective of memory, time, and "being in the now," one can see that these three "persons" always have the potential to be enlightened through different metaphorical frames and are not gender-specific. There is always room for one to play around and see *how three act as one* (from a slightly different but *similar frame of reference*!). Experimenting from a different intellectual starting point:

Memory extracts the essence that lived between two mysteriously chosen starting and ending points, as if what was between those *two* points was all *one* "now-like" story. The story of a memory is then placed on a wall for some type of *objective comparison*. After stepping back from what we have placed on the wall, we make sense of our past stories by giving them a *frame of reference* – a fitting border of appropriate color. Whether this reference frame is constructively metaphorical, deconstructively analytical, or just a manic struggle to find the right frame, there is still the same fundamental structure of the process of creating a sense of "now" through comparatively framing memories: The *memory holder* grips the storied past and holds the stilled narrative upright on the viewing wall (as stable as possible, or perhaps tilting and twisting to elicit perspective?). The *objective observer* stands back on what the memory holder has presented and becomes the blank palette for the artist who recreates the original within a new frame . . . The *framer*, from the point of view of the objective observer, finds (as the "*logician*" does) the fitting border—its shape and appropriate color—finally creating the truest sense of "now" that is the satisfying self-conclusion of fusing the past with the frame of the present that has now stopped, just for a moment, to be experienced truly.

Music – Speakers & Listeners:

Music incites the surfacing of latent frustrations[27] that have been set aside in the past for one reason or another. These latencies or emotional frustrations are found and brought to life through the company and witness of another, with music often serving as the provider of this witness – this "other".

Because music is the initial provider (or instigator) it can be seen as assuming the role of one's actor – one who speaks and feels (simultaneously) for you.[28] Music makes its way through one's person, but it is undoubtedly an external voice – a "real" *other* partner in shared creation. In this sense one draws the external voice inside oneself and lives through it as if it were theirs.

One might argue that the capacity to live "as if" or "through" is warrant enough to claim equal share of such life lived. The only difference between the two experiencers becomes the question—"who started it?"—a question known to dissipate, become irrelevant, or stall in ambivalence in the truest of shared experiences. In any case, we can imagine two harmonious speakers, in perfect mirror,

---

[27] They become evident through the uninhibited directions of mental recess, where "mental recess" means the receding of attention away from the external/unchangeable world of fixed objects, where narrow-minded zones, "clamp-downs" of categorization, and the anal-retentive delight in the clarity of rigid boundaries are left to rest, for the time being.

[28] I've been spoken for!

existing, without doubt, as simultaneous *listeners* to the song they both share to *speak*.[29]

The experience of sharing an emotion with another is the essence of self-discovery. There is no way to see the truth of one's emotional creation without presenting it outward, as a gift, for another see, have and hold in shared reflection. So the question becomes: who is this "other" that one presents their gift-of-self to? Do you see the other as All or One? Or both? Perhaps most importantly, when music has afforded you an emotional partner and a true sense of agreement, has the entirety of your person *completely* assumed the shoes of the "other?" Are you the equivalent of the other? Are *you* that All or that One? Or was that just a song – sung by an*other*?

When you assume the position of the other, without separation, you have unified your person to come together as both speaker and listener – giver and receiver of the ultimate gift.

---

[29] See section: **Speakers & Listeners**

SPEAKERS & LISTENERS

Of the various relationships between oneself and those who one chooses to acknowledge as being inside one's world, there are fundamental categories of audiences, or listeners, that define one's objective of communication and consequently how one speaks toward that audience. Often these relationships do not involve actual communication; instead we experience the presence of others as imaginary audiences, and we quietly test these audiences to see if our beliefs and attitudes might assimilate with them: Whether in the battleground of talk or the testing ground of thought, I, it, they, thou, We, and We All (One) exist as the subjects of all forth-and-back speaker expressions and subsequent listener reflections:

I : it – "I" recognizes an object as physical, impersonal, permanent, and of clearly defined boundaries. The first inclination is to give that object a name.

I : I – a two-person world where the distance between the two is equal to zero, that is, if the self chooses to be honest. The objective of this relationship is the discovery of truth and self understanding – reconciling the "I" and the "I" in the mirror.

I : thou – a two-person world of one-on-one: the other (thou) is believed to be feeling and conscious of the same outside happenings as you (I). The two are attributed the same quality of consciousness, as they share the same world. Any degree of separation is the result of hesistation or inability to agree or share truthfully.

I : they – "they" represent some external group, separated from yourself (I), whose mystery members are perceived to share some attitude about themselves and their relation to others in general. As far as that attitude is opposed to your own, the relationship of I : they is defined further by distance, opposition, and scruntinization.

I : thou of they – "I" acknowledges an individual ("thou of they") and engages so in communication, but the relationship proceeds cautiously with internally present world-view comparisons (possibly competitive). The relationship is usually skeptical to agree about anything or at least timid to agree about much. Ultimately an I : thou of they relationship turns the person (thou) into an example of the generalized group you (I) have associated them with, unless of course you come to appreciate their individuality without affiliation, in which case the relationship shifts to I : thou.

I : they of We – the speaker (I) shakes up the binding of the group: He has the desire to express his individuality by contrasting himself with some *other* person within the group. Hopefully, for the sake of the group, it is all in good fun and camaraderie.

I : We – the "I" who feels as if he is speaking toward or through "We" has assumed himself to be the leader of that "We". He summons the points of view of everyone in the group into what he perceives to be a perfect representation of those points of view, as they each and all feed into one another. It follows that the speaker, or leader in this case, develops a sense of guilt when his speech is in contrast to the feelings of someone who he wishes to include. The guilt relationship takes on the form of They : I . . .

They : I – He who is "they," the exception, the opposition, and in contrast is he who speaks against the "I" that represents the truth of the gathered We. He speaks against the leader (I) as a representative of they who oppose him. The feeling of being the leader of all who is they is a prideful one (devil's advocate) that has the extraordinarily extreme motivation to disassemble We into the impersonal world of they. The leader of We, on the other hand, who assembles and wishes to include everyone has the positive wish to see "they" as "thou" and teach the *individual* who represents "they" – *he* who is they.

We : thou (inside) – the collective attention of the group focuses on the truth of an individual who resides within and reflects the truth of the group. There is no relationship of type We : it.

We : thou (outside) – should the collective attention of the group be called upon to assimilate a new "thou" into the whole, the relationship takes on the form of We : thou (outside), where the entire group either speaks to represent themselves in hope of impressing their truth upon "thou" or listens with open ears to inspire he who is outside to speak and establish himself within the group.

We All : One – All have been collected – only to be imagined.

The Overseer, the Overseen, & the Overseeant

It takes the open eye of the Meta-Conscious to oversee what one happens to be doing. An idiotic mistake . . . "What am I doing!?" The open eye that desires to oversee *all* that she does inevitably develops the inclination to stop all physical action for the sake of complete observational oversight. She takes one step back from all happenings to the blank serene stare that lets all that is outside and happening impress upon her bare, unintentional surface.

The day of endless ambition breaks through when what the overseer sees herself doing is his act of overseeing in itself. **You,** the overseer, have now become the overseen: that previous, original state of oversight is taken on to be overseen by a new overseer of higher ground. This second, higher overseer of the first overseer that oversaw the original happening is next overridden to be seen by another rising overseer, and so on, and so on...one on top of the other, on top of the other – *ad infinitum.* There becomes a circular, rotational exchange of position that reflects perfect mutuality, where the overseer and the overseen inseparably rotate around the ultimate truth of all oversight, that is, permanence of self-being.

At such a phenomenal game of oversight, it is natural to wonder of who was the first to oversee?[30] No one. The overseer **is** the overseen. The two exist in such perfect rotation that their swirling sphere of endless "hand-pancakes," so to speak, gives rise to the Grand Being of Oversight—the **Overseeant**—She is, sees, and does all the same at once. She, at full ascension, sits calmly at the top – poised to descend on humanity.

---

[30] I know my thinker by knowing its habits of thought. The "I" that knows my thinker knows so much by having the *soul* purpose of seeing the thoughts of my thinker. So the thinker thinks, and the knower sees. The knower sees the thoughts of the thinker in order to know, and in his knowing begins to think some more—to recollect—so that, who knows, it all might come together. So the thinker inspires the knower, and the knower inspires the thinker – they are inseparable . . . now, who started it?

THE EXTREME HUMANITY OF THE JESUS CONCEPT

Pride Vs. Humility:

How and when did the supposed savior of the world **recognize** and cope with his own divinity? Blinded by the audience of humanity, how does One develop the courage, the audacity, to see himself in such a manner and put forth his purpose as being something divinely perfect or of another world? Such self-perception would typically be seen as delusional or mentally ill in some way; however, if there is such actual divinity or ultimate purpose to save, the embodiment of that person would surely not be subject to extreme delusional breakdown and/or social detachment. He must have had to contemplate his divinity through the terms of humanity, and in so doing must have been naturally presented with the struggle of all struggles when thinking or speaking his purpose – *pride vs. humility*:

It is true that we see ourselves in the eyes of others. And so He must have been aware that as He saves, He will be the savior in the eyes of others. Certainly these "others" would hold him "on high" or in special reverence. Even more certainly He will see this, of himself, and be overwhelmed – overwhelmed to an ultimate examination of self-identity, an examination so dilated, so engrossing, and so all-consuming of the moment in time when he finds Himself that it must have required nothing but infinite attention to all that defines the self—the lure of complete absence from all else—the pause of all pauses—a stagnation in the life of He who must act to save humanity. How does One pause such a game? And then what is the divine thought process that directs Him back to resume play?

He must lead the way to Heaven's eternal stage. In order to follow the leader, His people must first accept His end and direct their line of sight toward His way. Therefore the attentive direction that comes to consume all of humanity would be centered around Him, as He is the head, the leader, the mind.[31] And from this one might empathize with one of the ultimate challenges of His being human: *stage-fright*.

As the maturing boy first seriously entertains the emotional acceptance of His status as divine, the freshness of this notion is not humanly manageable. A human boy that is suddenly supposed to view himself as divine could not possibly handle this light in one take...So His first take marks the beginning of the long and recurring contemplative maturation that grows toward the full manifestation of His identity as acting savior and leader of humanity. As humans, it is possible to imagine His eventual saving grace because it is the same grace that is the essence of ultimate imagination and remains embedded as potential for all souls of humankind to discover – from His initial recognition of divine identity to the full manifestation and completion of the establishment of His identity.

But this is not to say that only He is divine. The untaught essence of *every* human soul *is* a perfect representation of divinity and a necessary link in the Body of Life. On the other hand, His role *is* a special one—of infinite responsibility—and this responsibility translated into the terms of humanity presents an amazing challenge for the He who dares.

The divinity that becomes perfectly manifested through His being is, in fact, within everyone, albeit latent. So it would seem inevitable that some will be tempted to entertain undisciplined hints

---

[31]   As He duked out the essence of all human battle, from extreme to extreme, He comes to represent the head, the leader, the mind of humanity as unified in the Body of Life.

to such latent divinity which may then lead to outward professions of their "almighty" status. *This desperation for efficaciousness and domineering wish to profess one's own divinity is the full-blown definition of pride.* Godly seen as Godly being, how does one incorporate this reality of identity without succumbing to the lure of excessive pride in awe of the Self?

In the case of *pride*, in which the person sees himself to have some special or important significance, there is a recognition of the responsibility that naturally accompanies such self-importance – e.g., internal dialogue, "the world is relying on me to save it, oh shit." That recognition centers judgingly around his thoughts and actions: he will feel as if the "divinely" prideful state of his person, as remembered by the past moments of greatness, must continue to manifest itself at all points of days because the audience of humanity, so to speak, expects the permanence of that "divine" position. The audience that is imagined to be "everyone else" and *counting on* the perfect order of his actions expects all of his actions to be perfectly divine. So, for him, there grows a fundamental layer of human experience that manages the duality of *self/external relations* and the perceived audiences that result and become expecting:

The first of two (no particular order) attentional experiences can be generally described as a rise of confidence where one gains a positive feeling of efficacy over the situation in which she engages: She is the *imposer* – her motives are pure in the fact that they are not scrutinized by meta-conscious oversight. Her intentions are perceived to be divinely flowing on a plane that apparently should not be interrupted as it coincides with the flow of the world. Her person is felt to be serving the positive expression of good purpose. This is the state of "free-flow" where self-assertion/motive/action all combine into one event where the person feels a sense of perfect intrusion on the external world as if to be the one leader in the face of the particular situation. She is the *imposer*.

The second of the two attentional experiences can be generally described as the most extreme burden of being *imposed upon*. The perceived attention and curiosity of others that seems to be directed toward the center of one's person is met with complete rejection: The person cannot think because any thought is metaconsciously recognized (by imagined others) as being suspiciously motivated, horribly ambivalent, and/or outside the will of his person. As diametrically opposed to the state of "free-flow," this is essentially a state of "stoppage" where such negative self-awareness marks a completely destructive examination and stagnation in the ability to act within a social audience:

The presence of *other minds* is existentially inexplicable—it can't be proved as any attempts at causation links exist in fantasy—and the presence of these *other* points of view is often rejected as an external threat to the pureness of one's self-identification. There is, in a sense, a reverse dilation of attention toward the field of self/external relations where the person retreats from the confusing presence of other judging minds to a destructive (deconstructive) state of self-examination, where no thoughts are allowed to pass through the all-judgmental meta-conscious censor (toward physical action or external expression). This state has the ultimate goal of death – the complete disintegration of the person's will to be, act, or express the essence of their person in the light of others.

On the other hand, the rejection of the existence (or significance) of others can be conjured into a positive feeling if one allows pride to be on their side. While the confidence that accompanies pride is often necessary to explore the entirety of one's being and one's unlimited potential to be a lovely creator, the end lure of pride is, combined with human nature, the most extremely negative lure and temptation:

In the face of had-been-latent beauty and realization of self-worth, the infinite Love that breaths within every soul can come to the attention of the Meta-Conscious and overwhelm the person. Then, the lure of pride can take such a recognition of one's beauty to an end that projects oneself as divine, only this path demands that only *you* are divine – the *one and only* person who possesses infinity and screams to go on and profess the glory of that identity as being superior to *all others.*

What pride will never tell you is that he is leading you down a path *whose* end is loneliness. Pride separates oneself, in all *your* glory, from everything that is human: set above, you have no companion, and when the glory subsides and the need for relational truths sets in, you will tumble and disintegrate.

Both the man of pride and the Man of humility have looked up to the sky to discover their potential. The man of pride, through the power of fantasy, sees this potential in the sky and ascends himself, in special reverence, to an imaginary cloud that hovers above humanity. The Man of humility looks up to the potential in the sky and conversely wonders: does *everyone else* see this . . . is everyone else *with* me? So in the tricky game of pride vs. humility, the question becomes: Is everyone looking up *to you*, or is everyone looking up *with you?*

As is for all humans in the face of temptation, he comes upon us to make the choice clear. His face—the face of temptation—offers to tell us everything we wish to know. Some will immediately fall, and others will think twice but never be sure of which side is ill and which side is eternal . . . So is the looming question that the One struggles to put to rest. In constant search of answer—something seemingly impossible to arrive at through His mere human person—He wonders of who is *h*is savior? Who or what might elicit the rise of His latent truth of being?

The task appears so unbearable—so impossible to be taken on merely from the human within—that there appears to be no agency of internal motivation that can make occur the ultimate occurrence. At this lack of will He looks *outside* himself for that thing, that moment, that someone who might make things click—clicking to finally have undoubted inspiration to take what is inside and make a whole world of it outside—when give-and-take is pure and the World is ready to receive. So is she the World? Or is the world She?

So is the typical straw. He/We become caught between two directions. Both seem to be essential – essential to our survival, essential to our truth, and essential to what is right to follow. So in this lifetime—this meantime of ambivalence—to choose right is to not choose at all. The point *for now* is that the choice is yet to be made. Yes, the choice *will* be made, but not at the exclusion or repulsion of one side. Now, to make the right choice is to be acquainted with both sides – not to banish or turn away from one, but to bring near and come to the fullness of what each side represents. After all, in the end it will not be so cut and dry, with clearly labeled sides . . .

Ambivalence:

During most of daily life one's attention is torn in all directions yet required to maintain its focus on one. Only sometimes does one have the chance to wander and wonder about from where all these directions branch off. In other words, most of your life you have your back to God. But still those moments always come when you might turn around and say like, "What up Be? What Be dis?" Obviously it's not that specifically verbal; more so it's like:

When you're filling up a water bottle at the water fountain and someone is waiting behind you in line, but you weren't aware that person was waiting; so when you turn around, there is a crisis of direction. Usually the person behind you steps or leans to one side or the other so as to lead your choice of direction, but it's not so easy when you turn around to say what's up to God. He doesn't lean to one side or the other; He stands right in front of you, no matter which way you go. You lean one way; He leans the same way. You lean the other way; and so He leans . . .

The ultimate lesson here is that it's never so cut and dry. When you turn around to see that there are two directions to choose from, God never leans one way to make the choice clear. I mean, Christ, if we knew the consequences of an action before we took it, it wouldn't be too hard of a choice . . .

Hello there expired human #4893256840. Choose *this* and you will be in pain for all eternity . . . Choose *that* and you will be in Love for all eternity" . . . That's not even a choice! Can I get a witness? . . .

So the Child exploded from the Original? He blasts forth to be the secondary witness to what *was* (hmm?) *before* he left. Bound by the past, tortured by the present, and in Love with the future, He says "OOOh, give Me what makes the three One!" In this desire to be the unifying mediator, He is the *active* imagininator who serves as the through-point between what was, what is, and what will be because, after all, there surely is no difference.

He creates in reflection of the Father's originality, ultimately culminating *from* and *through* the point of view of the end, looking back in wonder to the ultimate understanding of Our point of origin. So in the presence of time, We wonder how the beginning differs from the end, and what requires such painful existence if the *two* are essentially equal and dependent on each other for ultimate *two*-way reflection. Here and now,[32] why must we play this game?

---

[32] Now is never what it seems. After all and only after all can there be a permanent sense of "nowness." The now of here on earth—the here and now—can only be captured through noticing difference between *two* points in time, that is, by holding in memory an experience that has already passed and then examining the quality of that experience from *another* point of view, removed in oversight and playing the role of the objective observer. The point becomes that there is no "now": All "moments" have already passed, and there remains only three that hold their ground, as exemplified in perfect balance and the aura of permanence: the Experience Holder, The Objective Observer, and the Gift that is re-collected and assimilated between the two.

The game of *back and forth*[33] is away from the Father; you can feel this. But it also feels as if humanity's glory of redemption is dependent on *both sides* of the game – through the two sides' sharply perfect contrast emanating eternal co-dependence, mutual understanding, and equality. So then, does our redemption require us to choose one side and proliferate its goodness into eternal life, effectively ending the game? Or does His saving grace have culmination involving more even-handed deliberations – more so an understanding through co-eternal perfected reflection, that is, sustaining back-and-forth rather than destroying it…becoming harmonious with time and no longer a relative to pain? By unearthing the integrity of both sides or, in other words, reconciling the tension of differences, is humanity's slavery to pain and disintegration (death) ended as time ends? Is it true that we require our opposite for perfection of complementarity? Does black and white combine to produce a gray throne of neutrality?

If the Savior represents the defender of Truth, His role as defender must be in the face of some opposition. Successful defense—His identity as savior—has never been in doubt from the Father's perspective, as what is eternally true has always and will always be true. In other words: *it has all been done before.* Therefore His identity as defender is dependent on those who oppose his defense and eventually become "won over." The nature of co-dependence is the seat of His humility, but in the presence of time, distraught by the apparent absence of unification, His job on earth is clear – to unify. The hardest part becomes temporarily discarding such humility

---

[33] "hopping back and forth" can be enlightened through a host of different words and phrases, but one can describe it basically as the wicked ambivalence that accompanies the perception of a pending choice. Choices are illusive – they will come through the back door and out the front before you know it. You might think you heard the door slam—that someone came inside—but that was just him leaving. Or sometimes an option will be so bold as to stand right in front of you. And even when you choose against it that same option is one step ahead, still right there in your face when you turn around. Jeez, how did he get to the other side of me that fast? I thought I was ahead when I turned around to leave him for good?

in a self-recognition process whereby He comes to believe that He *alone* bears the Truth of mind to unify *All* in the Body of Life. He reaches out for All but knows that All have not yet come together to join Him. So at this He knows He must leave and return[34] to introspection . . . alone.

Alone, He transcends limits of self-knowledge and grows at a divine pace, discovering the heights *and* depths of humanity. As introspective moments culminate, He brings with him more latent truths or "missing links" that had been lost in shady depths. Inside and out until He has found everyone . . . . . . Here we are still . . . the last must be devilishly stubborn.

Once & For All:

"Once and For All" is the height of all fantasies that always seems to fade before becoming clear. After all, we surely can't give away the ending! Again we are left with a strange uncertainty or ambivalence about our ending that we are left to play around with. So forgive me if I, the nameless narrator, begin to trail off and present *hypothetical wonders that do not really conclude anything but hopefully evoke the appropriate, applicable emotion that might place the reader on the proper precipice . . .*

To assume responsibility for the safe return of all lost souls—all those who have tragically fallen—is to have the weight of the world on One's shoulders. Everyone's fate would depend on His steady, willing hand of grace, so the last thing He would have make sure, to be eternally sure, is that *no one* has been left behind. He, as leader,

---

[34] One might see this as symbolic of Jesus' *two* trips to earth: A perfect son tries once, has something or someone to work on, and learns from that first trial. "He returns to the right hand of the Father" after crucifixion. Feeling forsaken at first, He *thinks twice,* then returns to earth for one more try. The moment before leaving He knew he would be on his own for awhile . . .

summons and collects *All*[35] to be assembled in the Body of Life . . . just one missing link will stave the Kingdom of Heaven on Earth.

The tragedy of the Savior is that it is His personal assumption—His essence of being—that He must save One and **All** when, who knows, some might have to be let go. Some funny recurring dream tells me that there is a stubborn "last soul" who appears to be a toss up?

The frustration remains until We **All** agree. The one who refuses to make the leap to agree (who we can call "the fallen one") will exist as long as someone agrees with him, and so the game of frustration will continue. The game continues as long as there is someone on the side of the opposition, so we can sense that in the presence of such a two-sided game that, at present, many still agree with the fallen one who represents the opposition.[36] The end the fallen one promotes is death, and through his persona of such a perfectly stubborn refusal of life, he tempts all to follow him unto death. None of his followers have yet died because (for now) they remain loyal by his side, awaiting the final battle and the cause to call *everyone* unto death. So in the end everyone will be or not be, depending on which side is turned . . .?

Which brings us to the other side and He who represents the leader of All into life – the Savior: He sympathizes with the stubbornness of the fallen one insofar as they both share the same dedication to their side of the game. With perfect humility, He has as much sympathy for the fallen one as He does passion for life. The soul/sole function of His gentle hand is to turn the other side, as the story goes – All will follow Him into life . . .

He leads the front of the line and shepherds the back, making sure all are accounted for. Of course, in the end, He looks back to

---

[35] The only question becomes whether or not you have the heart to embrace *everyone*. Because as you begin to ascend, if you have to stop and denounce someone, anyone, you will be gone – unable to catch up with the height you saw, wished, and knew you could reach . . . think again.

[36] "I hope you guess my name." –Rolling Stones

find the stray loner—the last to remain—and as so the final scene on earth begins: At this point, with no one on his side, the last to remain (the fallen one) must choose with eternal implication between life and death. Judging by his nature,[37] it would seem he is inevitably headed down the path of death, and so it begins to look that way. As the last to remain begins to pass away, the Savior cries at the thought of a final farewell and is frantic to revive. Essentially, a spiritual mouth-to-mouth takes place, as life attempts to breathe into death. A moment of self-recognition leaves the dying one whispering, very serene-like, "quit trying to resuscitate me." How is the Savior to respond? . . . It is the hardest of all things – to *live and let die*. As the Savior sheds a tear, the dying one says farewell and cheers to a good game. If it were not for his parting words, the Savior could have cried for eternity; newly inspired, He turns back to His people and heads the Body of Life. The Truth of the game and his passed friend stay close in memory. Can this all be true, or might the Savior have brought the dying one back to life?

---

[37] If I am doing good, then I do not know it. If I was before I was born, then I am, and I will be. If I was not before I was born, and I – in the now – cry to choose, who or what is my guide? My guide could only be the endless consequence of all consequences, when truly only one choice was made – a long time ago. So I see that maybe I was not before I was born, but maybe I was at least simultaneous with my birth. So he who is eternally dark cannot be judged. His only point of return is through our hope and openness. If he turns away, simply wave a nice goodbye. At this he might decide not to leave.

Author's Notes

These notes might give the reader further insight and direction toward the discovery of interrelated themes and tactics of author presentation.

Certain sections have presentational objectives that are diametrically opposed to those of other sections. Certain sentences shift from one objective to the other as to remark on the quality and contrast of that shift. This multiplicity of presentational objectives might be seen to play together in a peculiar kind of game.

Themes recur, and as these themes are written to recur, they often appear so (the second time) in an evolved, matured, or just an elaborated manner – a manner that often reflects the very recurring theme that is, at that point, being read by the reader to be recurring. It is often that intellectual logic and creative emotion take part in a seesaw battle where, afterward, they might look back on their game and say "cheers" to their creation of symphonic battle.

POINTS OF REVIEW

Character Profiles — Habits of Speakers & Listeners:

Each character profile reflects a general attitude or mode of speaking one's mind. The consistency of that attitude throughout the discussion is not what happens to be most important, as it is surely not perfectly continuous through each character's expressions: The attitudes overlap, here and there, as each character is ultimately trying to uncover the same latent truth while dealing with different personal obstacles. Each character simply *tends* to indulge certain habits of speaking for complicated reasons. Most important is to recognize and understand the different attitudes at work and how certain imaginary audiences accompany their speech. In general, the attitudes are these:

David Manifold: dangerously clings to the heightened awareness of "I" — a heightened awareness that is dependent on his extreme creation of "they" who stand in contrast to his exceptional "I." His exceptional manner of individuality creates a very personal world of words, that is, he often crams too much meaning (that only he can understand) into single words or short phrases. His cramming allows him to experience much at one time but is somewhat unhealthily dependent on "they" who do not understand that cram fest (but should, in his mind), and so he speaks in frustration.

<u>Prescott Bookman</u>: devotes himself to the truth and heightened awareness that comes to life through the binding of We. His putting forth of general lessons, as if to be a teacher, is his desire to have truth of being be emotionally relevant to everyone. He is all ambitious to agree and unite with others, so his speaking reflects his assuming the role of the leader/teacher of many (all humankind) – all of whom he imagines will unite to agree with him. His motivation stems from that imagination of agreement.

<u>Martin Overfield</u>: cultivates the heightened awareness of "I," but its growing identity is self-reliant, unlike David. His concern becomes self-understanding and the self : self relationship (I : I). His narratives reflect the desire to know the story behind one's soul.

<u>Jimmy Simpson</u>: exemplifies an adolescent resistance to the homogeneity experienced when one succumbs to the true sense of We. In other words, he is distraught by the thought of losing his individuality in the homogenous experience of agreement between minds. He knows the truth of We, but is tentative to release the individuality of his childhood that had always defined himself though competitive distance (I : they of We). In this sense Jimmy plays a dual role in the discussion: His camaraderie establishes a sense of group and community, but he also makes sure that the distance between individual truths does not close too quickly or capriciously. He mans both the wall that encloses the group and the buffer zone that keeps them separated within.

<u>Peter Clearville</u>: essentially serves as the intellectualization character. He often utilizes alternative vocabularies that translate otherwise emotional discoveries into more sterile contextual frames. In this sense, he takes the We All : One relationship (that creativity inspires) and strips it of all emotional seams in order to see that "whole" in terms of its pieces (I : it) – pieces that fit an unemotional frame of reference.

The Afterward & its Relation to the Discussion:

The afterward takes somewhat of an emotional rest to contemplate the breadth and complexity of those emotions that were achieved in the discussion. In looking back on those moments of creativity and emotional revelation that lifted the discussion into being, the afterward captures, organizes, and elaborates on interrelated themes that were at times intellectually disregarded because of emotions that were all-consuming in the discussion.

Themes were *emotionally* gathered and interwoven during the discussion. In other words, they were more so *felt* to be streaming together than they were intellectually recognized and recollected as such. The afterward in that sense moves forward to discover the creative discipline needed to soak in the feeling (and be soaked) and then intellectualize the profundity of such feelings into better organized worlds of verbal thought (drying off).

There are some key points to keep in mind when reading the discussion, relating it to the afterward, and more importantly when reading the discussion + the afterward again, and *again,* jumping back and forth:

- The discussion was created *before* the afterward, as redundant as that might sound: In a beforehand time of creative self-discovery, the discussion, in its lack of self-restraint, planted seeds of understanding. Creative ideas and the emotions that accompanied them were bundled in excess and all experienced to be true at single but dispersed moments in time. In these bundled moments there was not enough working memory capacity to dissect and fully integrate all ideas into some handle-able understanding or tighter intellectual framework. The *"moments of truth,"* therefore, crept back up, as motivated by creative guilt, for further contemplation and intellectual work to better handle . . . into the afterward.

- The intermittent "intellectualizations" are premature (pre-afterward) first efforts to "come down" and gain emotional stability. In a sense the discussion was beginning to stumble upon (through instinctual adaptation?) what was necessary to maintain a grip on reality while still being far removed in a world of unbelievable beliefs.

- The scattered footnotes are elaborations felt to be appropriate that would have otherwise disrupted the flow of the main body if they were entertained within. Often the footnotes represent shifts from an intellectually presented idea to a more emotional presentation of what that idea evokes in true experience of feeling, or vice versa.

- The only particularly *intentional* part of this work is this part – the author's notes. The discussion and afterward, on the other hand, were all part of a continuous following of a feeling and reflection.

Finally, whenever there is no clear direction, such as when I am wandering around my apartment or daydreaming in class, I tend to fiddle around and play with stuff for no reason. When I let myself go like this, sometimes I am lucky enough to gain insight into what's going on behind all scenes—the theme of no direction, all directions—the un-translated dream:

And I was in class the other day, resting my head on my arm, fiddling with my pen in hand when for "no reason" I started poking my pen down on this book of mine to stop the back cover from opening up by itself. I would press down on it briefly with my pen and then lift up to watch the back cover open back up again (all by itself!). My "play-child" saw the lesson was clear: When a book has been open for a long enough time and you try to set it face down, thinking for sure that you have finished that book, the back cover will always open back up by itself – to remind you that there is something more to this book: your story is not over . . .

www.ingramcontent.com/pod-product-compliance
Lightning Source LLC
Chambersburg PA
CBHW050356290526
45786CB00003B/1005